Digital Artist in the
New Century

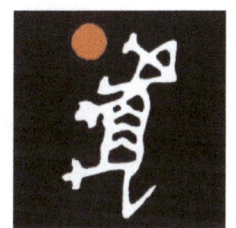

Gloria King Merritt

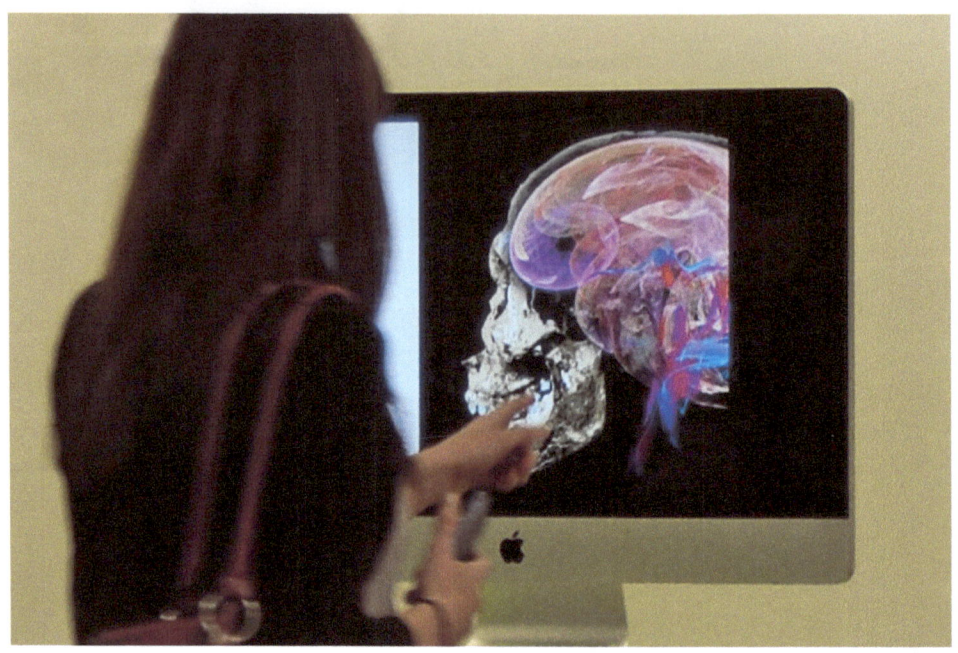

Digital Art by Gloria King Merritt on exhibition at Massachusetts Institute of Technology in 2013.

www.GloriaKingMerritt.com

First Edition.

Published by New Media Access 2013.

ISBN-13: 978-0615929040
ISBN-10: 0615929044

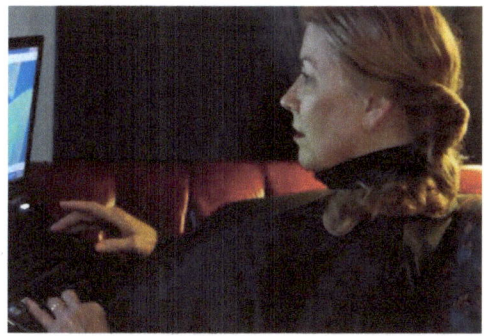

"Every generation invents a new artistic technique or medium to create new ways to express the concepts, thoughts and feelings of the age. The painter's brush is an extension of the hand, just as the computer is the extension of the creative mind.

I was trained by a series of talented artists in a variety of disciplines and encouraged to investigate the breadth and depth of virtually every artistic medium, including drawing, painting, metal, dimensional resin, photography, video, and color theory.

The symbiotic relationship between Master and Apprentice is one of the oldest ways of learning known. The Master Artist spends a lifetime experimenting with materials and pushing the inspirational envelope.

For the Master, the consummation of a complete creative life is to pass on this hard earned understanding of techniques and become the source of inspiration to their chosen apprentice. With this education, and the emotional support of the Master, the Apprentice sets forth to create a new fresh body of work.

Digital art is the most contemporary fine art."

Gloria King Merritt

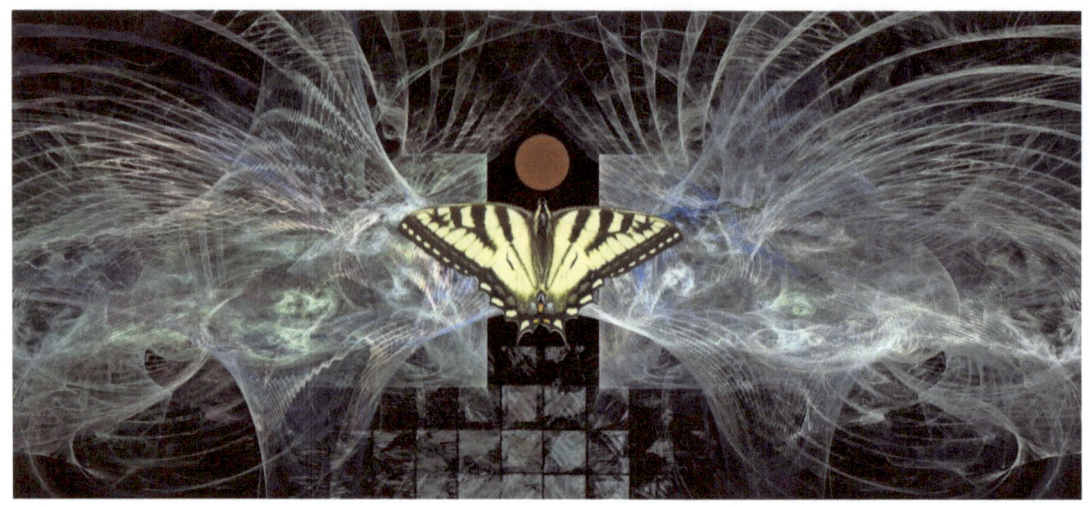

Butterfly Effect – Homage to Lorenz

Edward Lorenz, an MIT meteorologist and Cambridge Massachusetts resident who
worked to understand why it is so difficult to make
accurate weather forecasts, succeeded in unleashing
a scientific revolution called Chaos Theory.

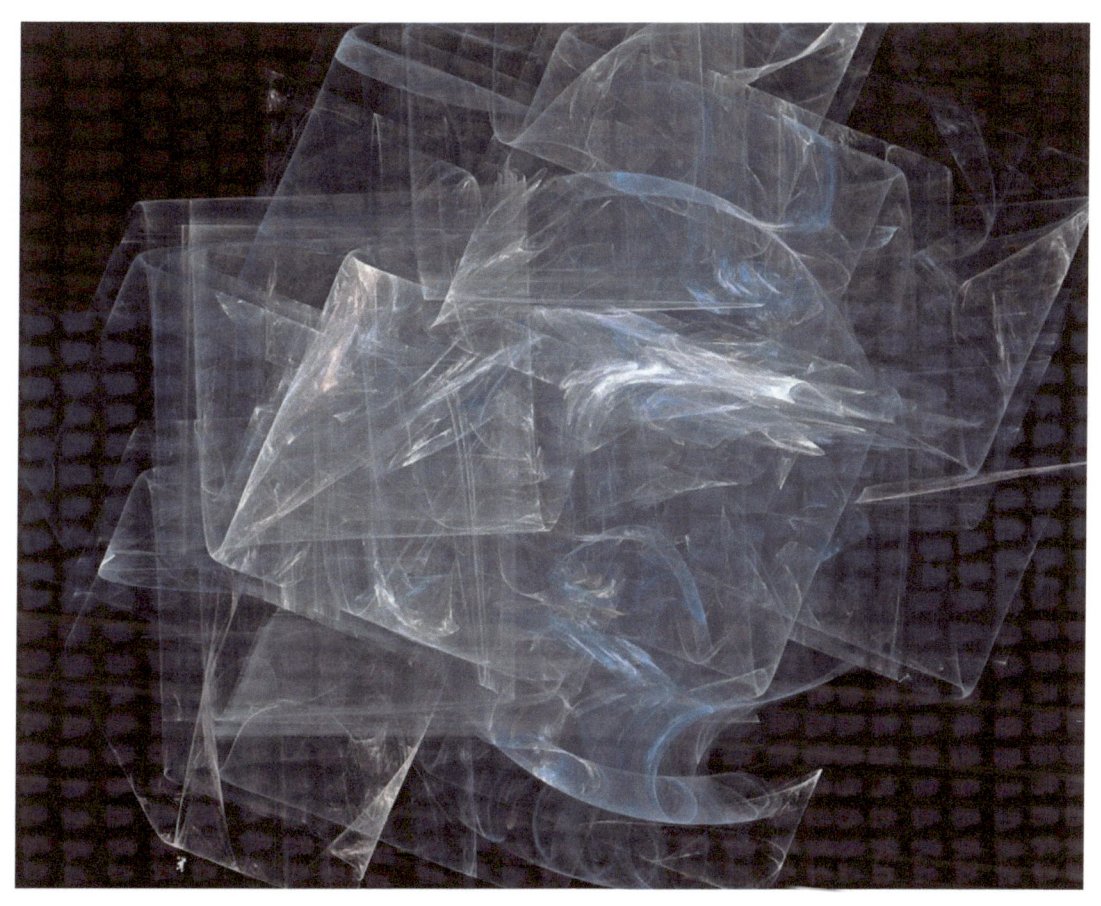

La Cellophane

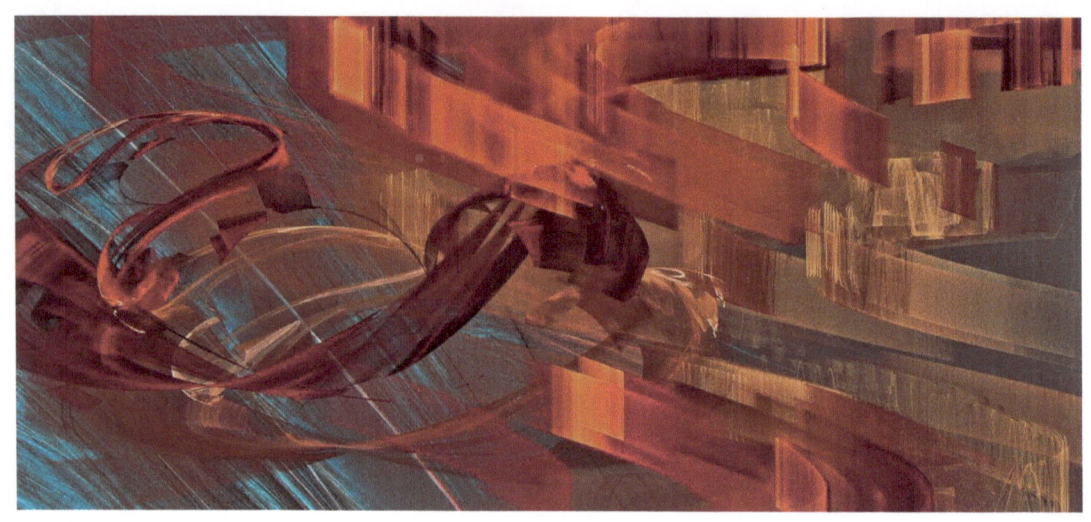

Red Ribbons

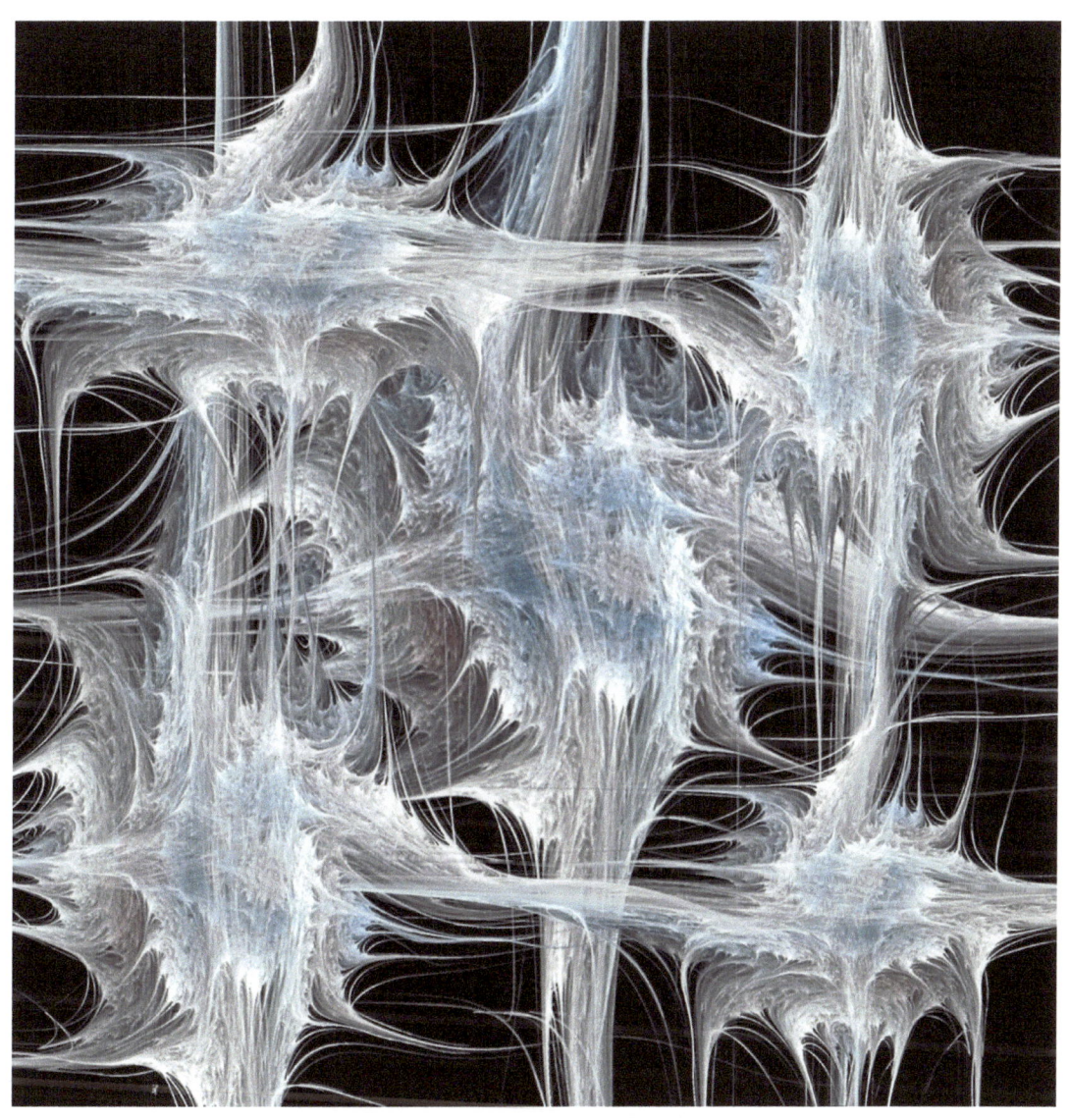

Very Gooey

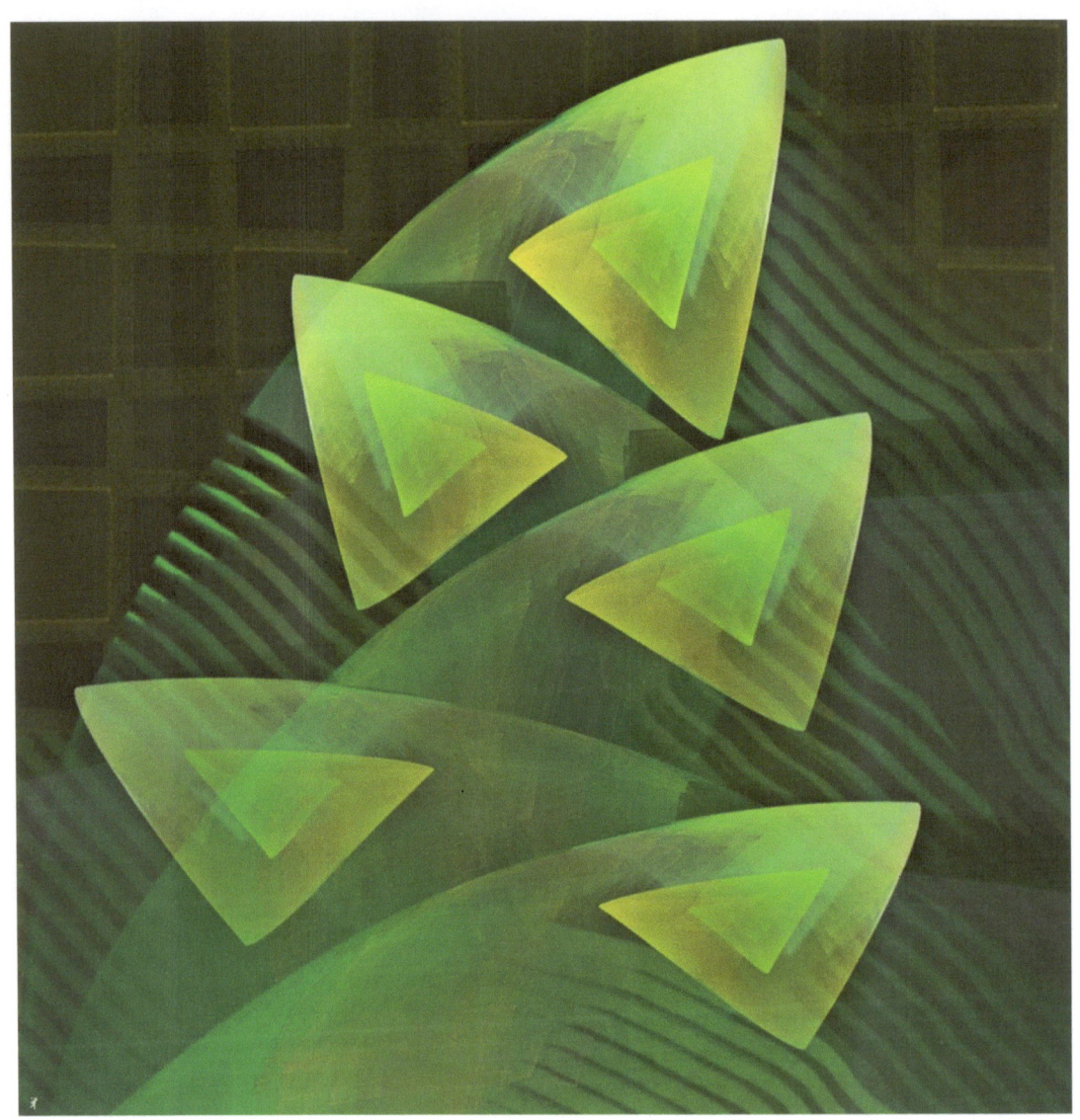

Fiddlehead Ferns

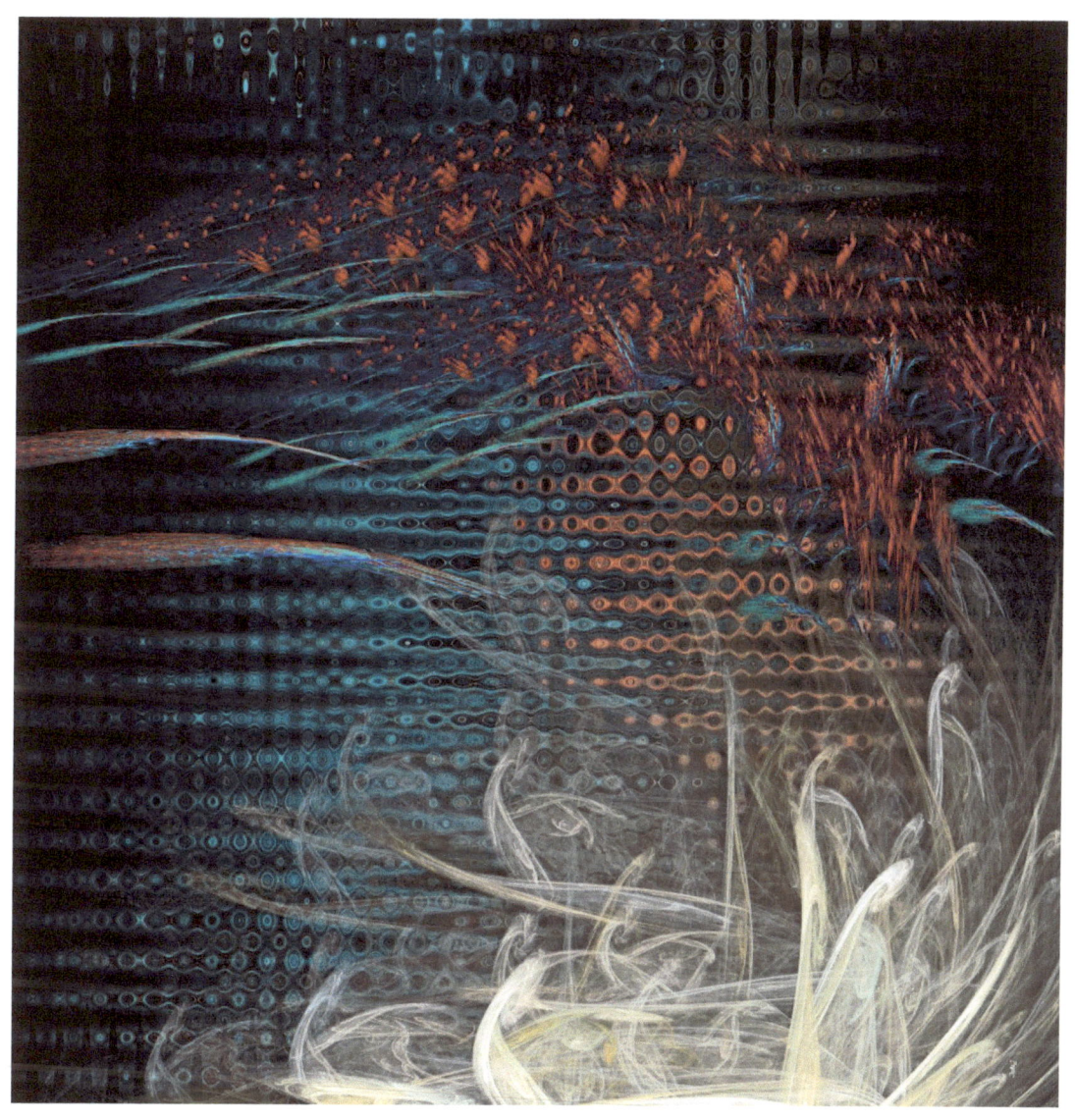

The Spawning – Eggs and Milt

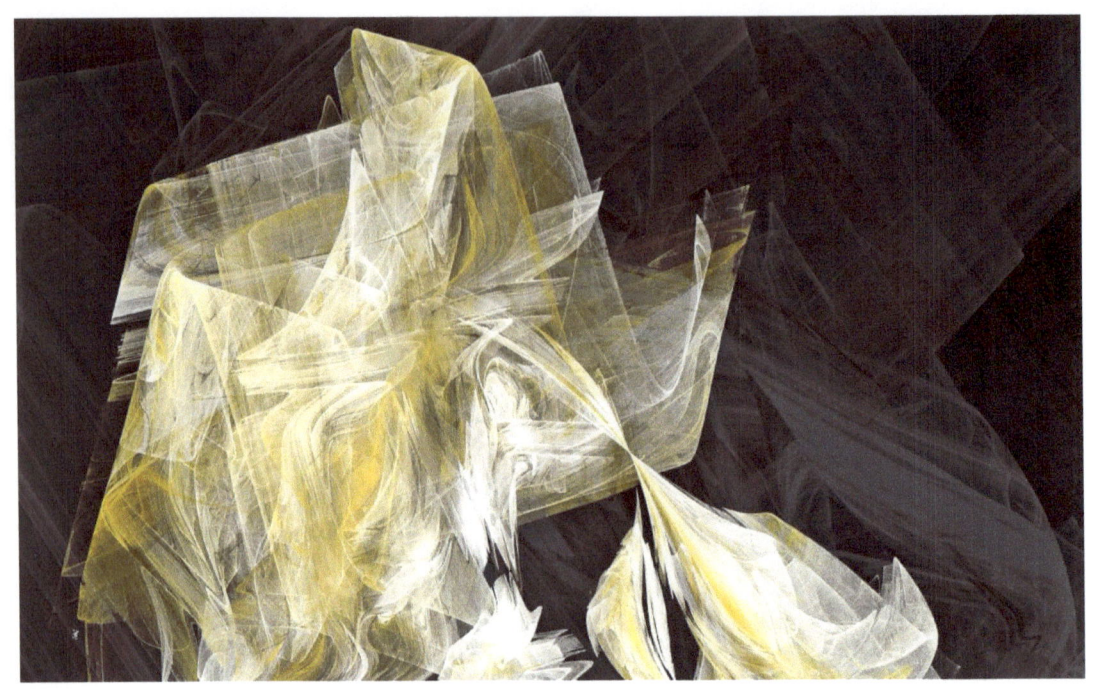

Gift Wrapped

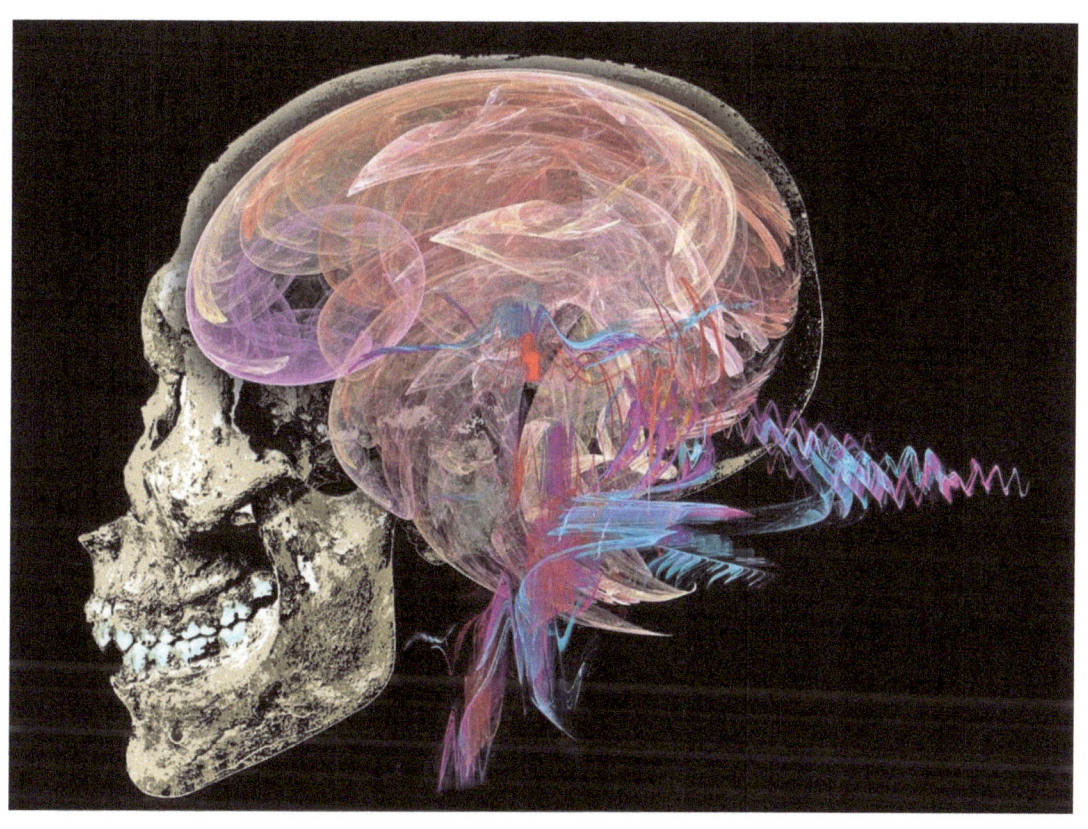

Blue Tooth – Wireless Communication

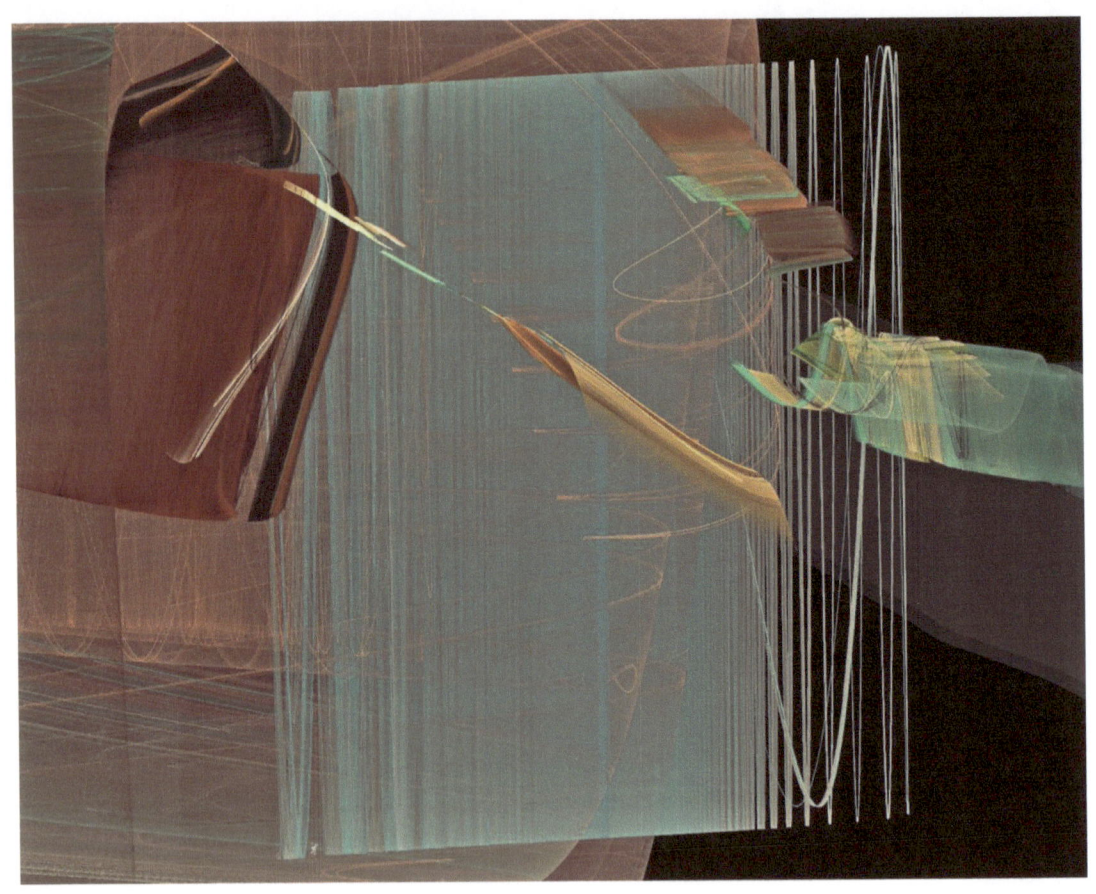

Mahogany and Teal

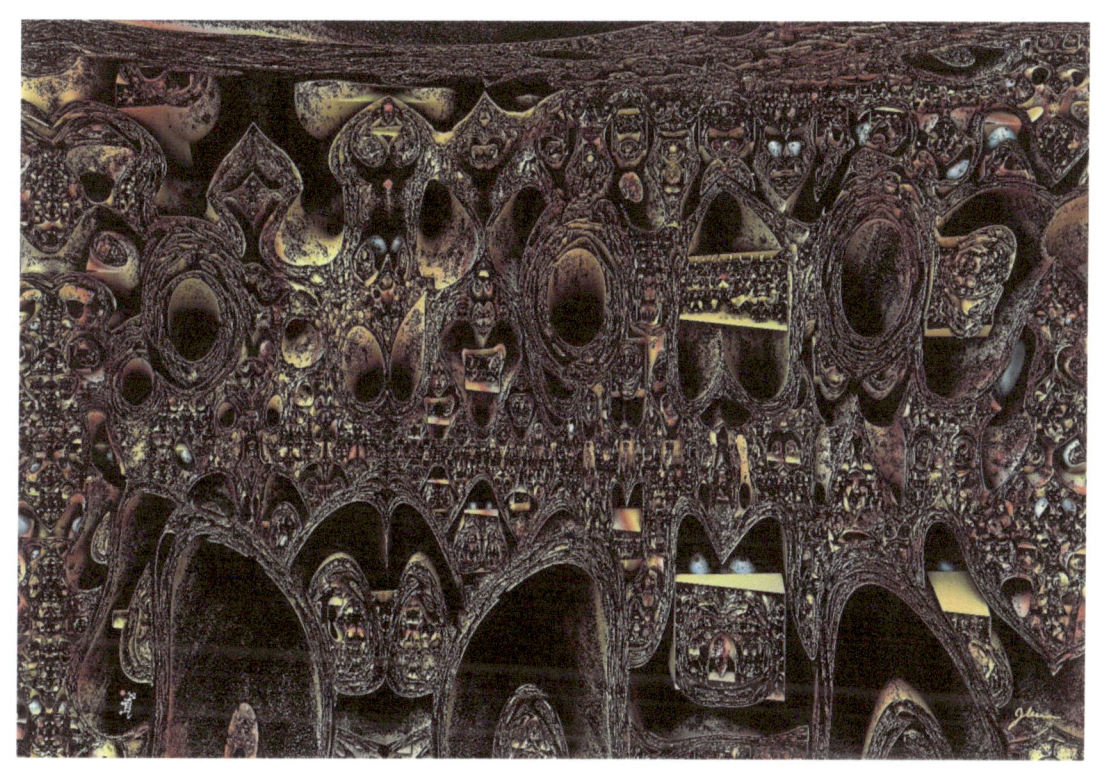

Scroll of Life and Death

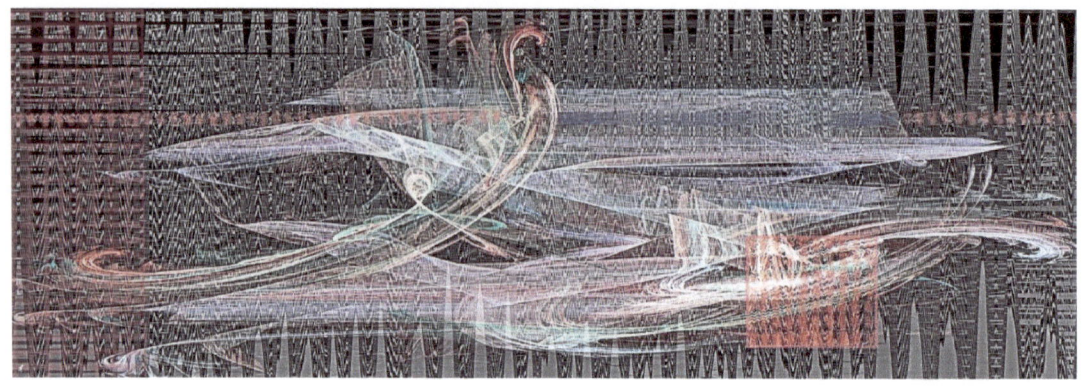

Pulse Rhythm and Song

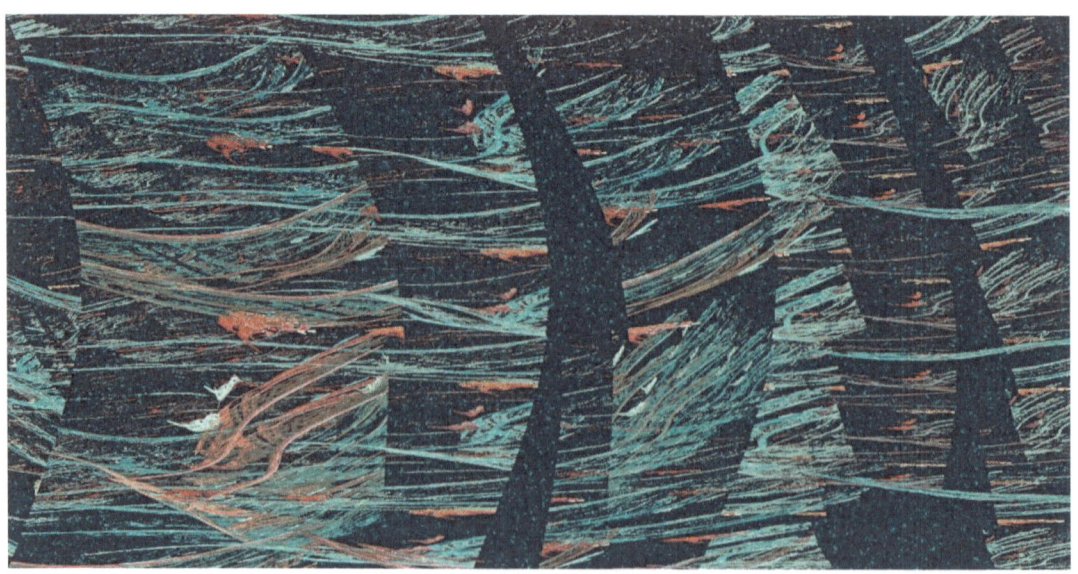

Swimming Upstream

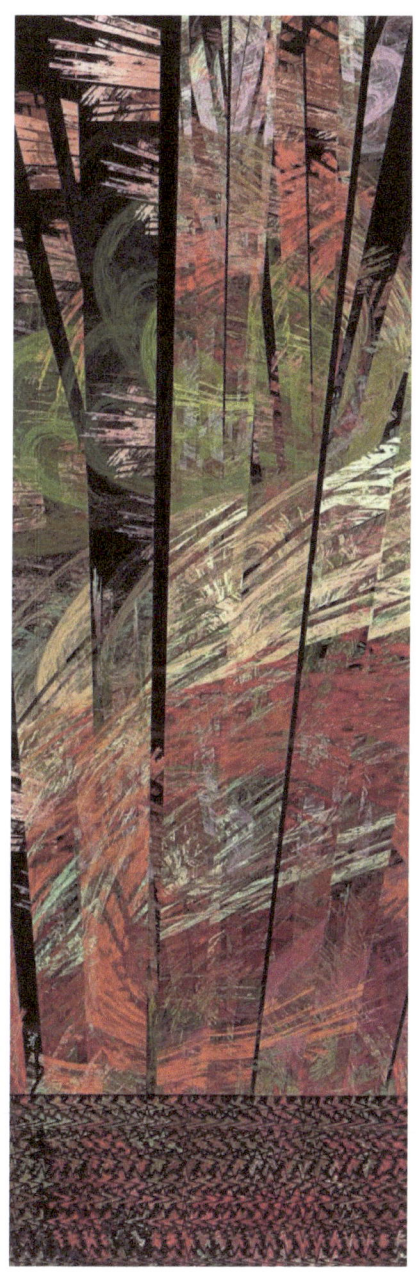

Jungle Grasses

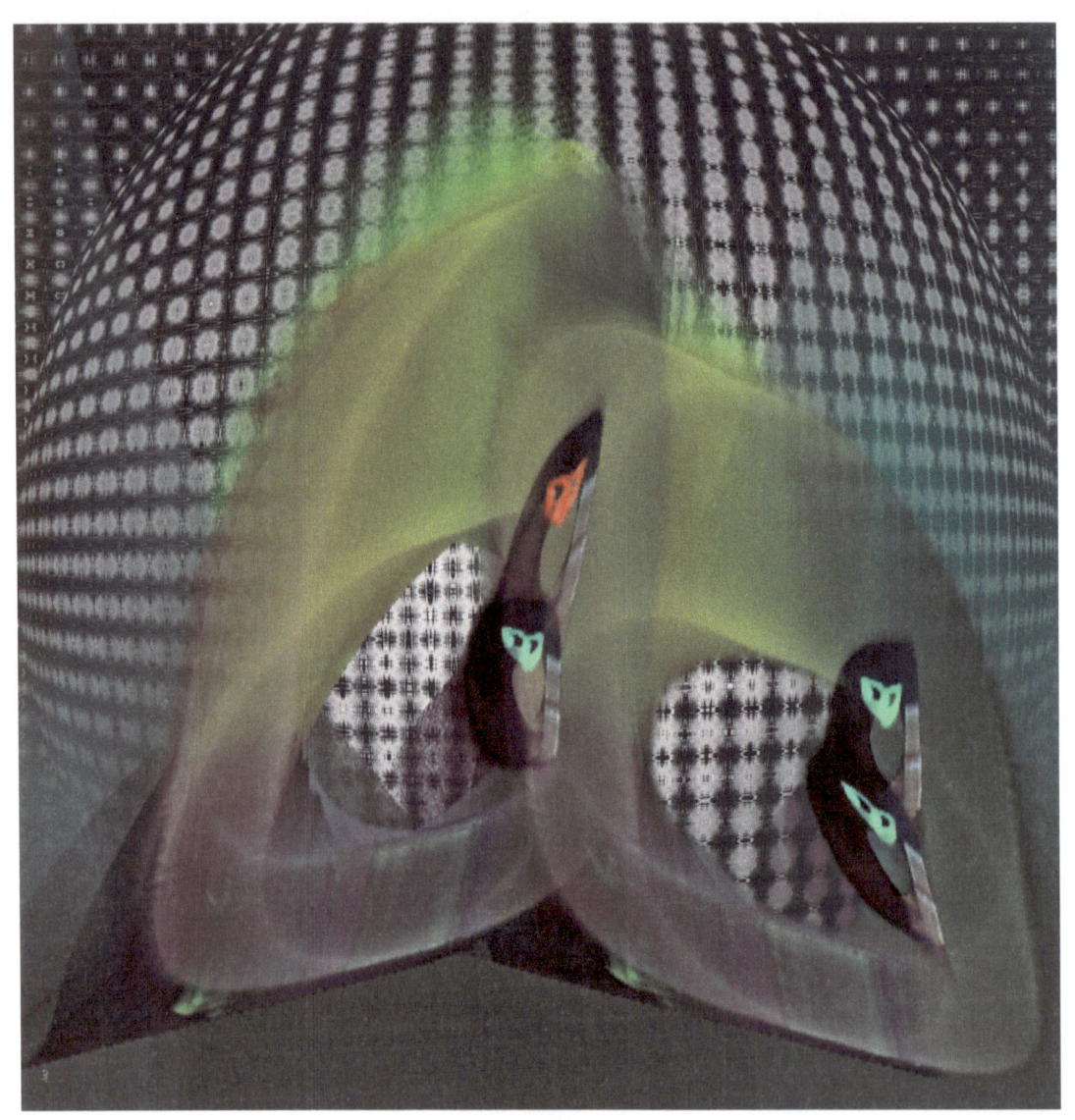

Seed Matrix

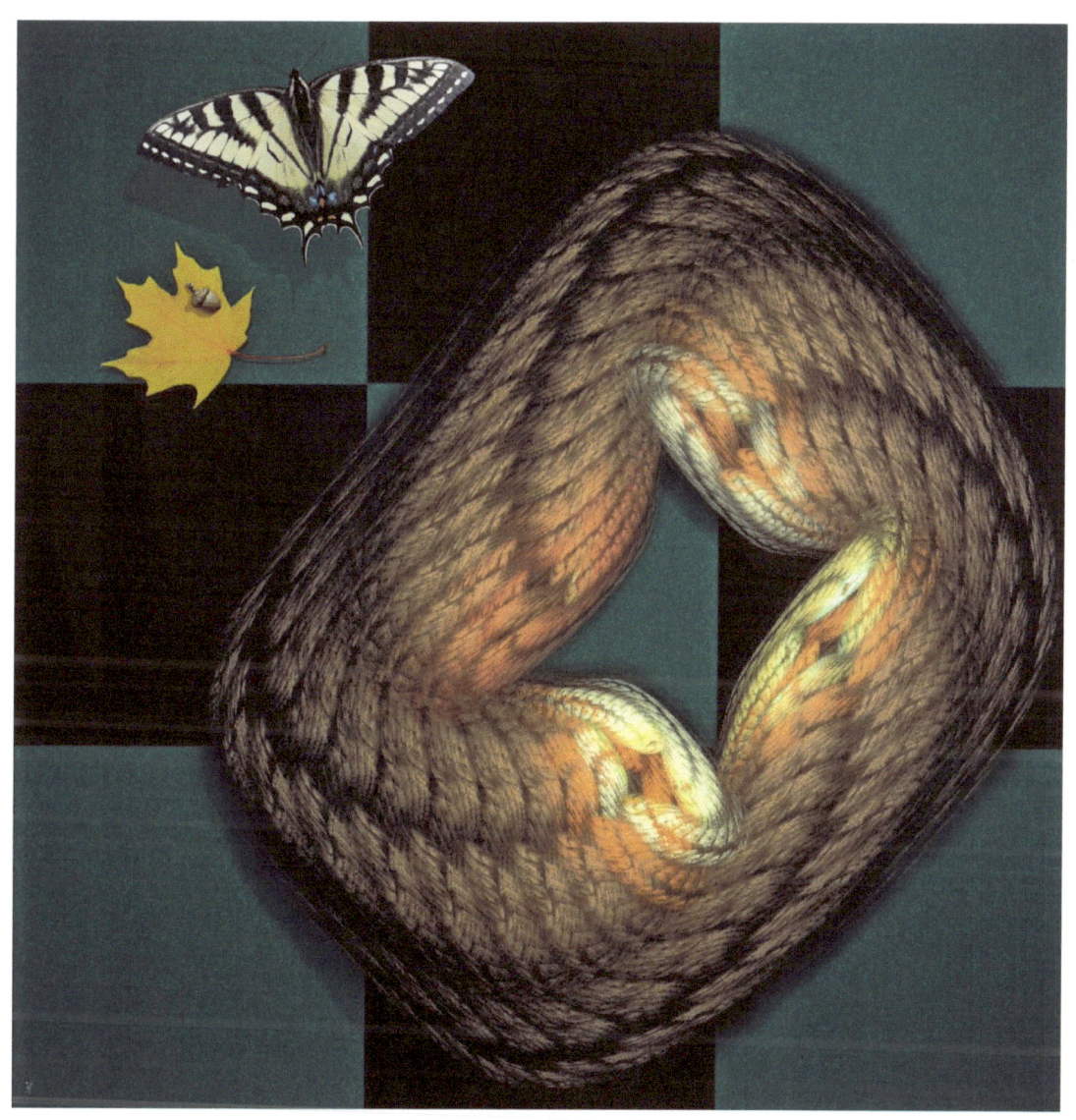

Eternal Ouroboros

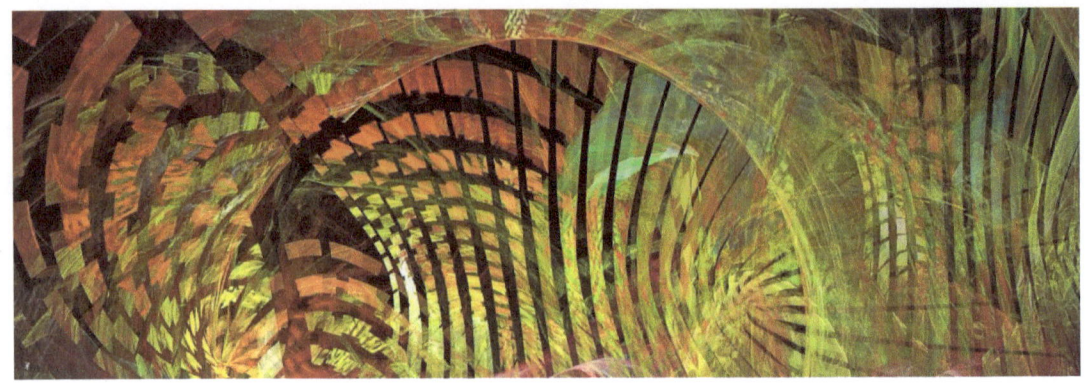

Welcome to the Jungle 1

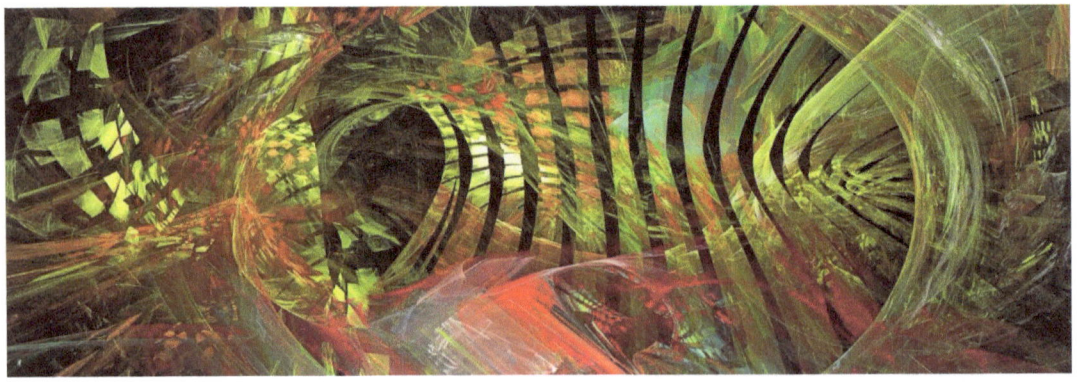

Welcome to the Jungle 2

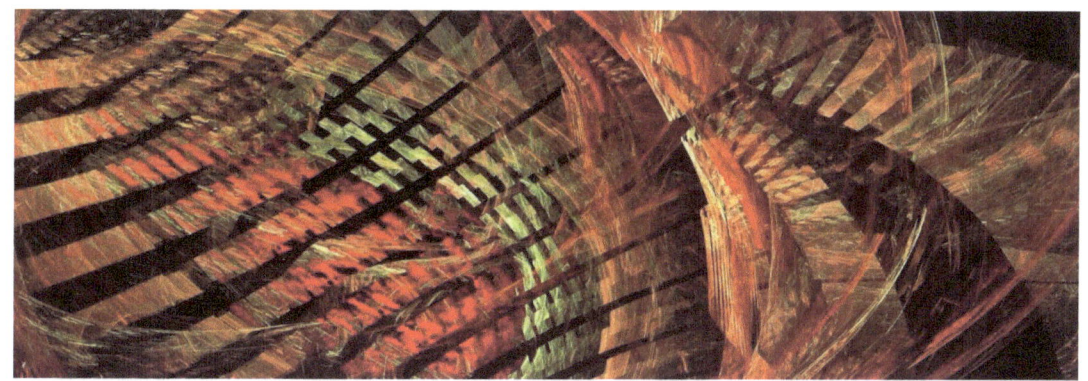

Welcome to the Jungle 3

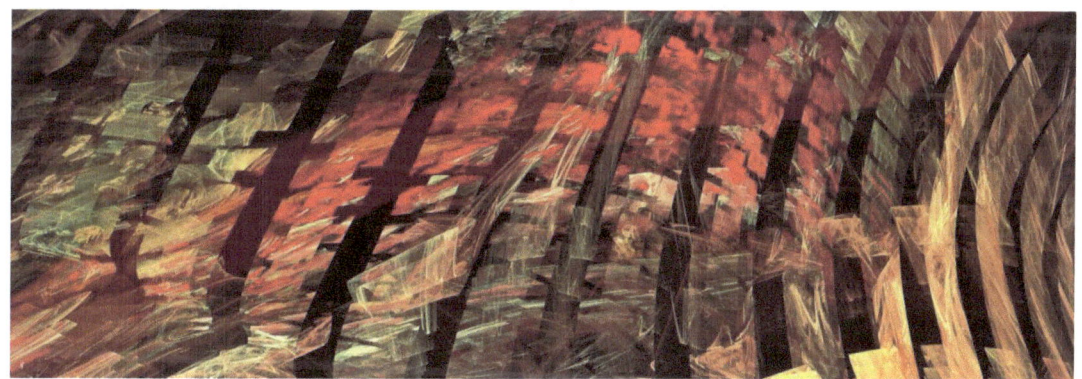

Welcome to the Jungle 4

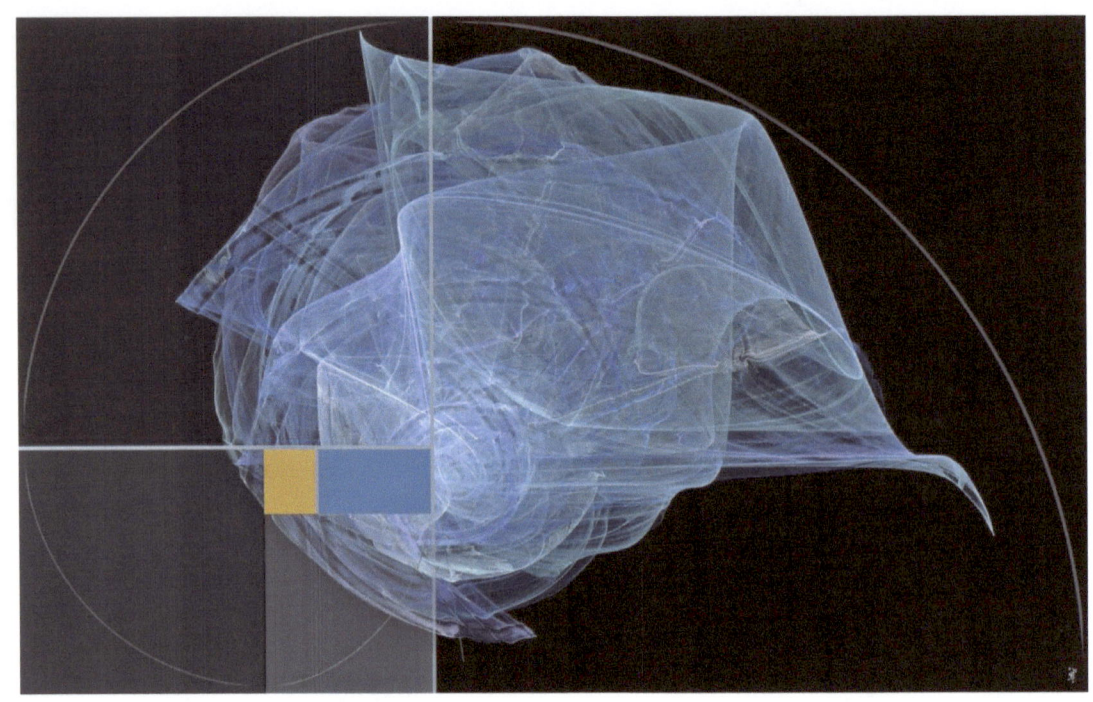

Divine in Chiffon

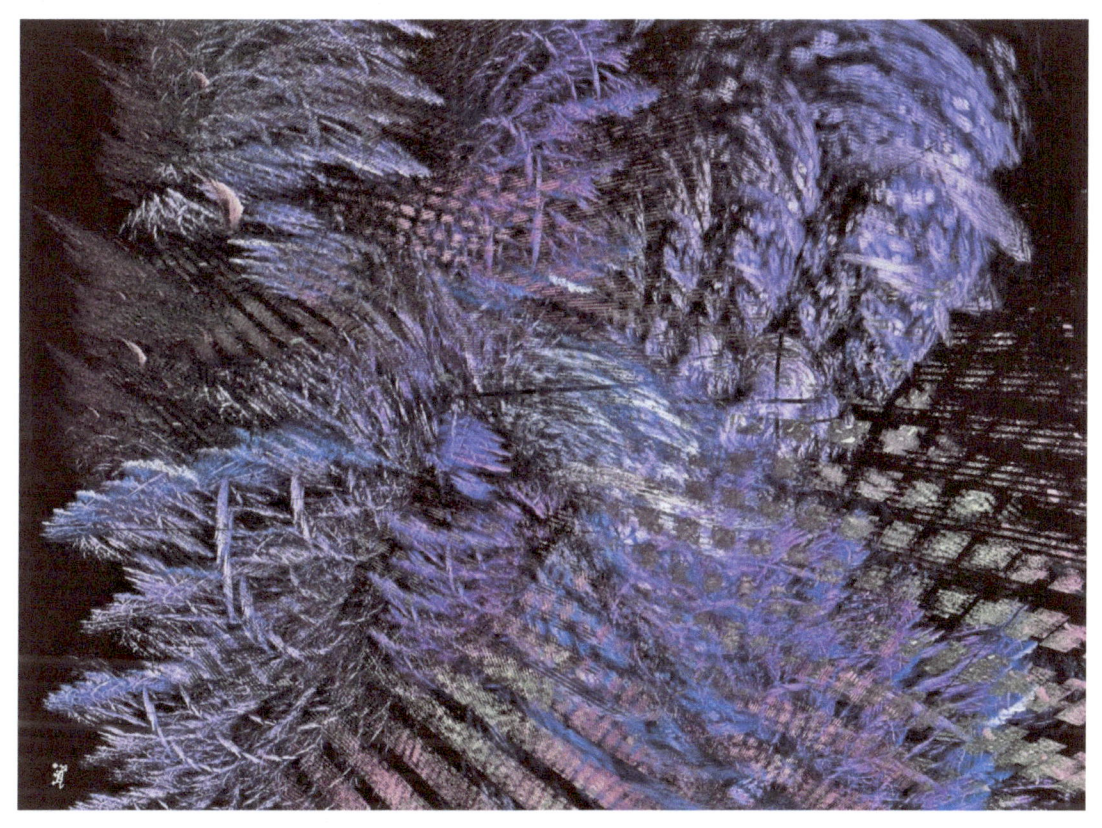

Knot that Binds

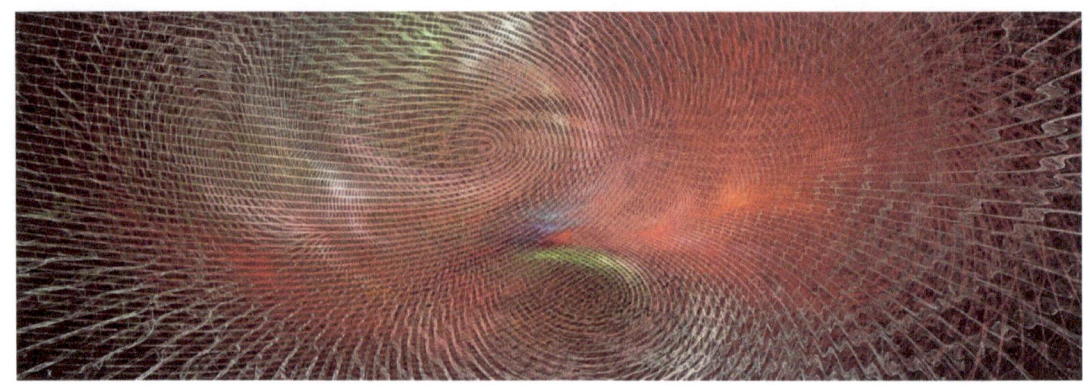

Universal Fingerprint

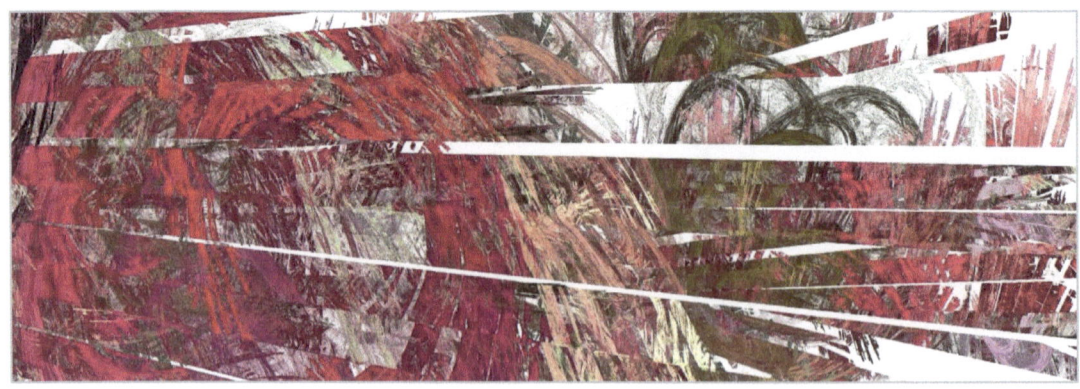

Welcome to the Garden

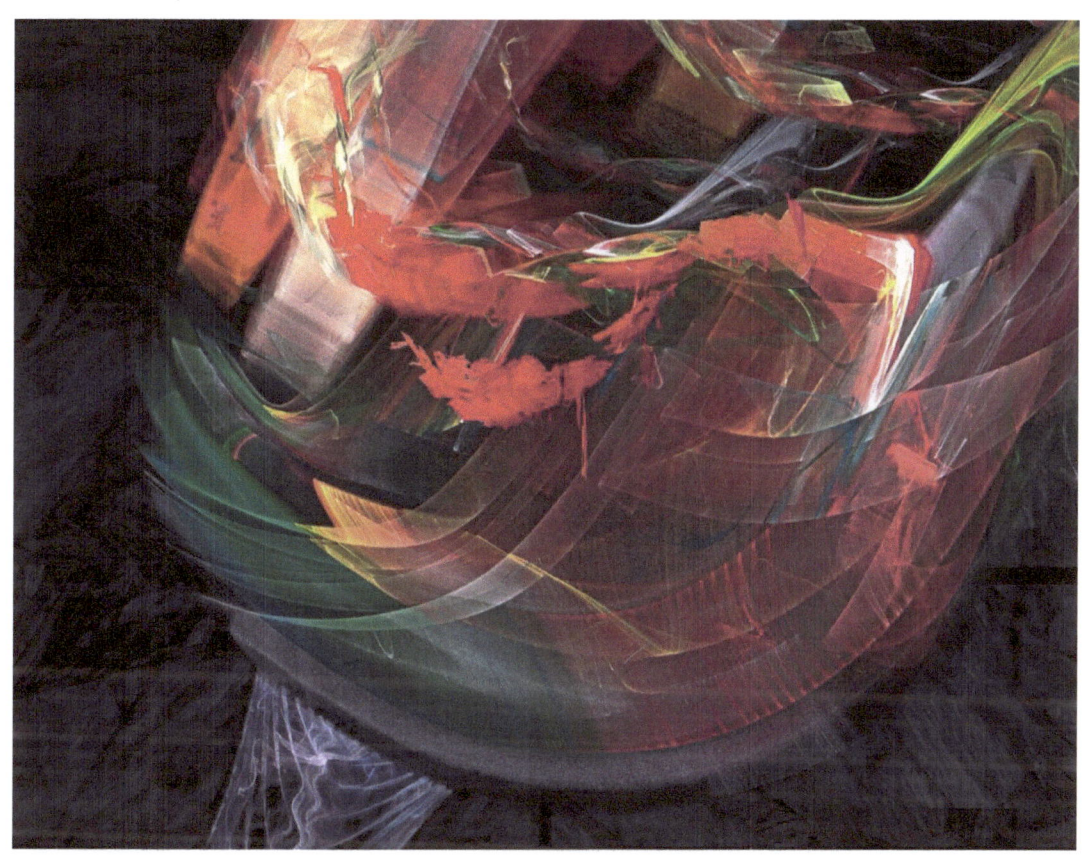

Complex

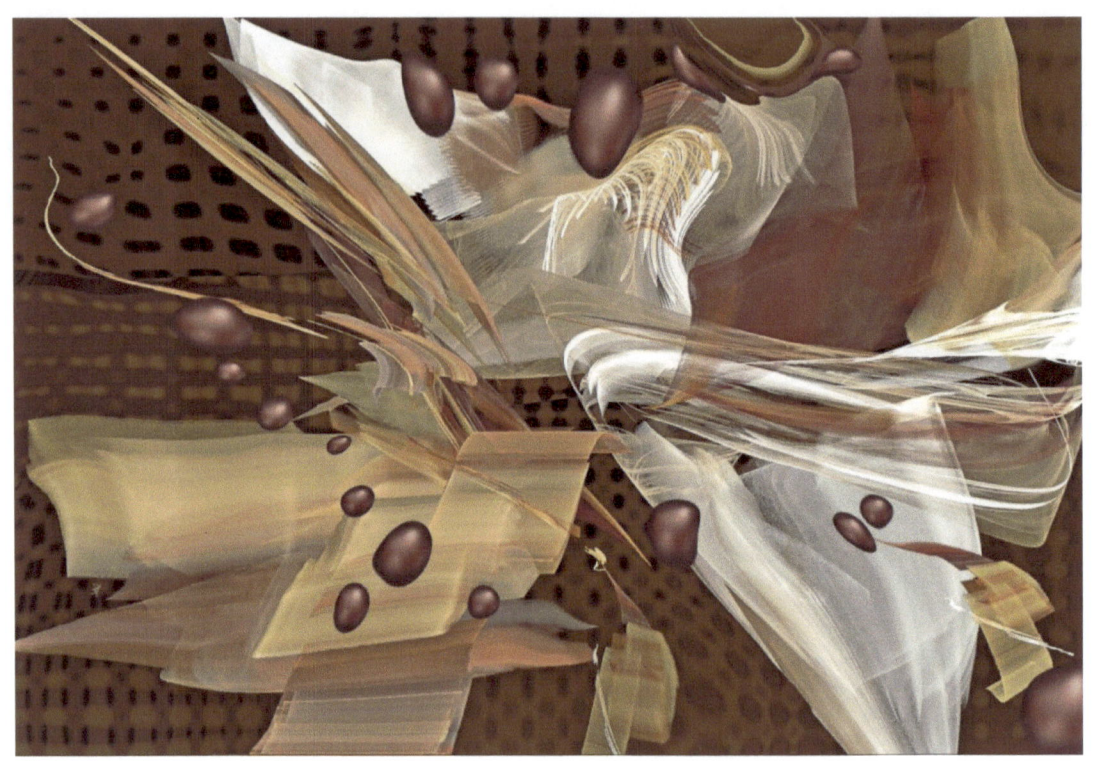

Painting with Chocolate

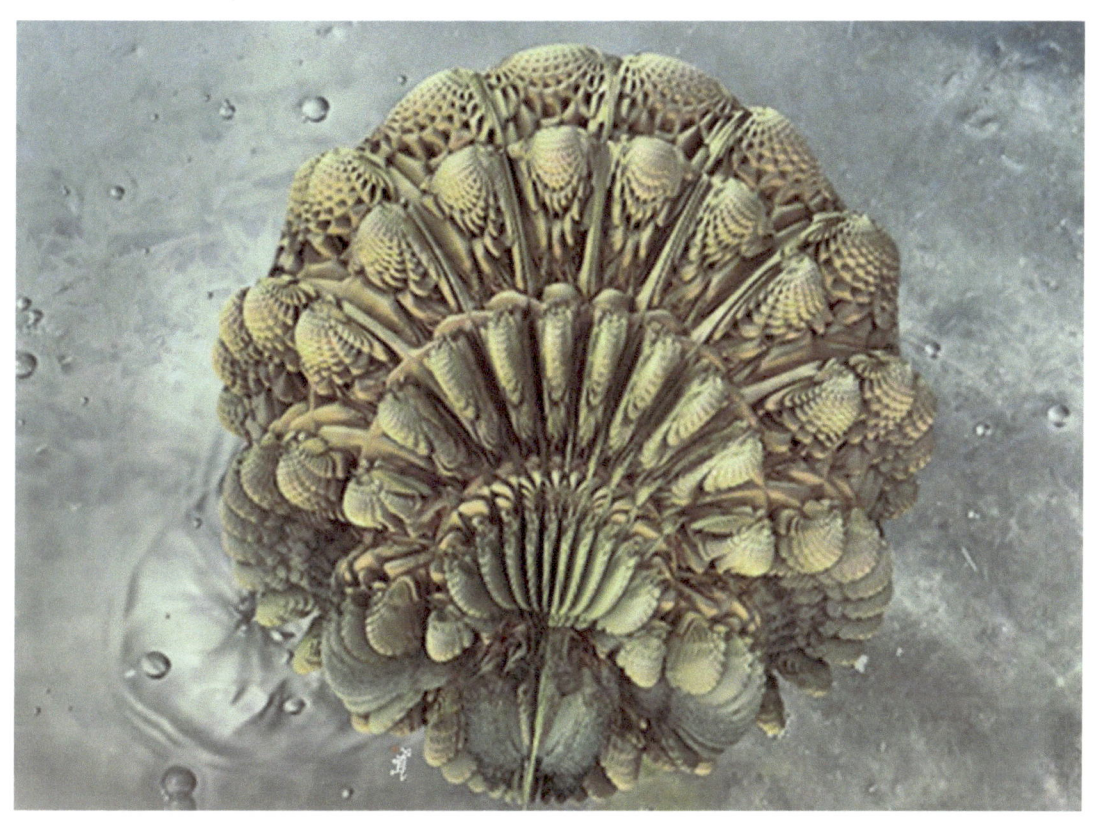

Ancient Ocean

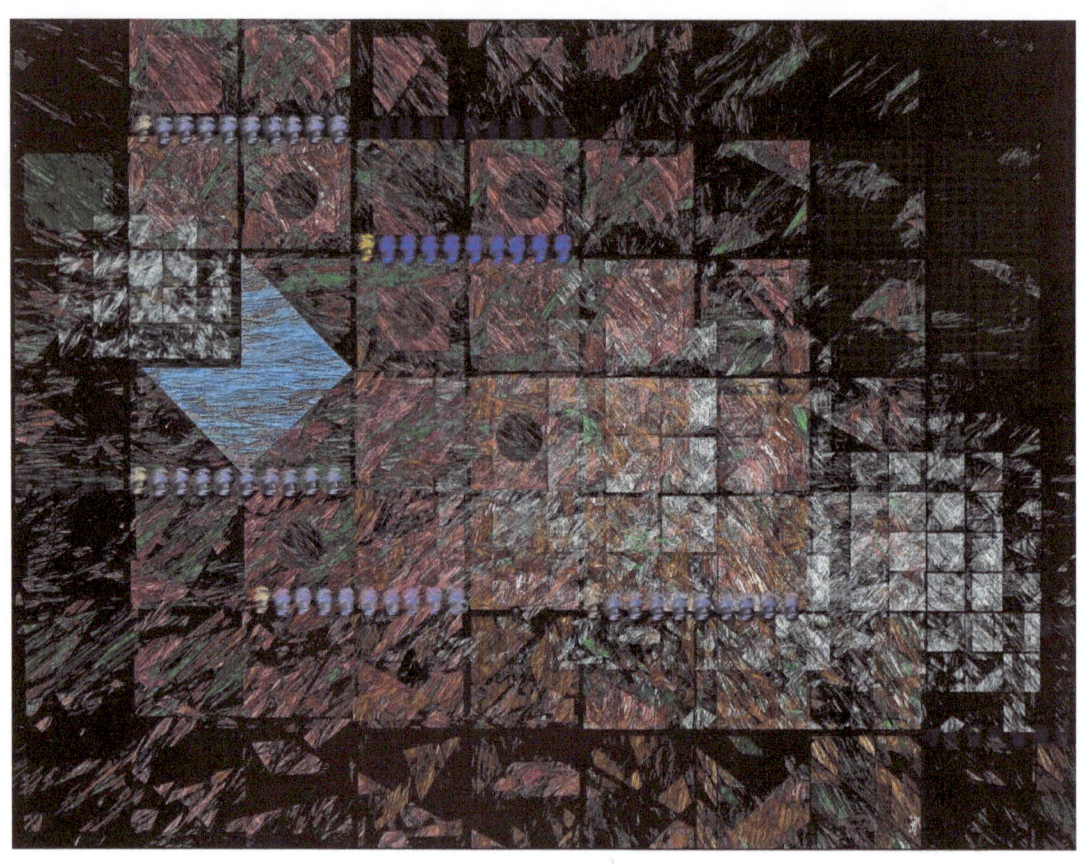

Stitched Together

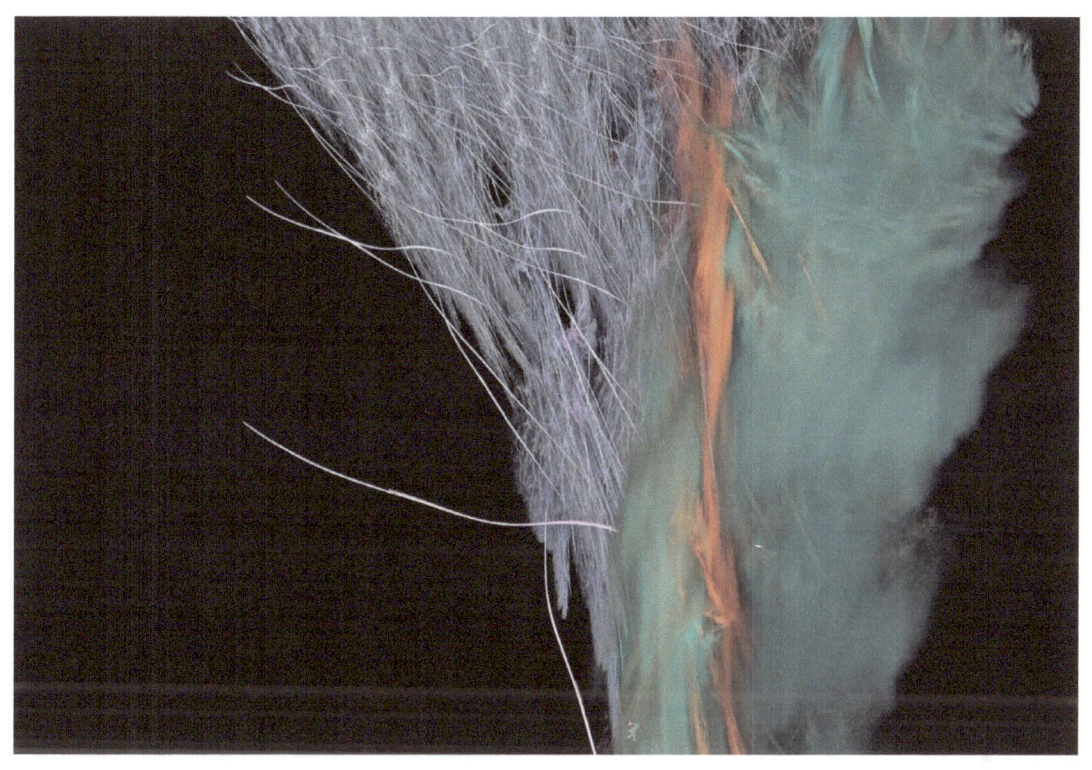

Kindling and Flame

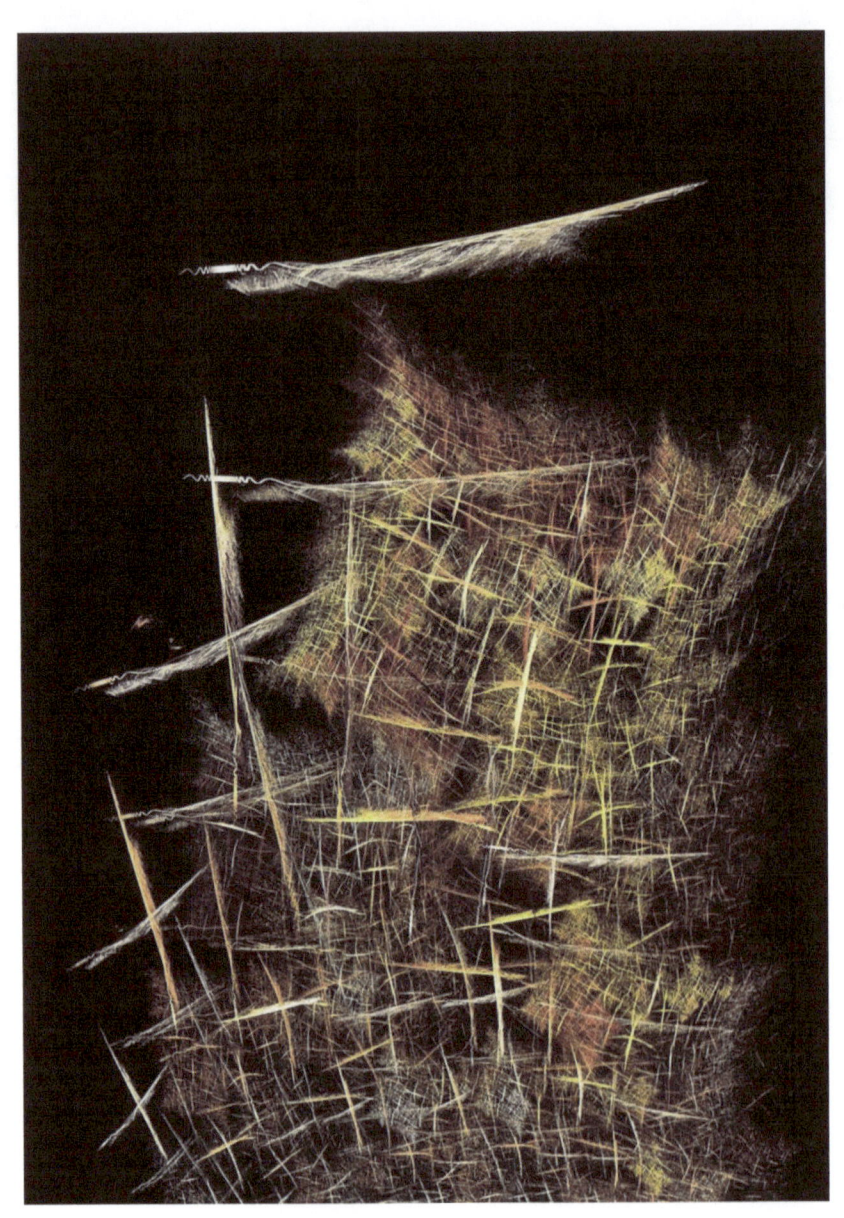

Feathers and Wool

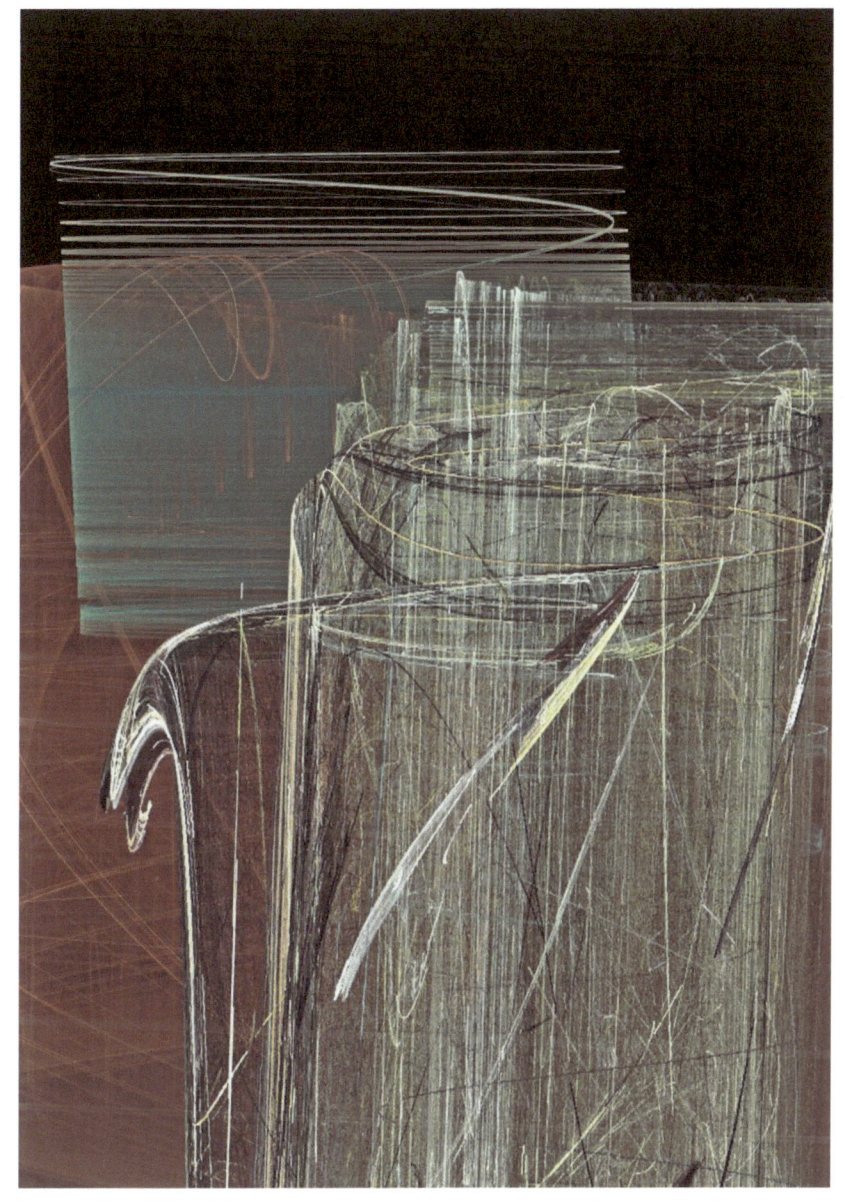

The Glass Pitcher

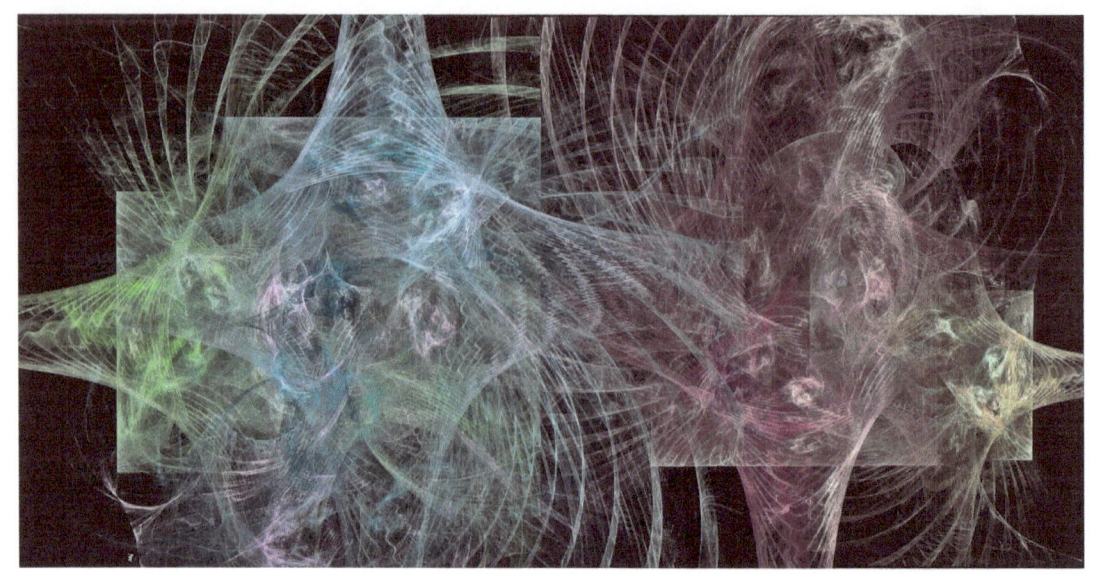

Room of Sound

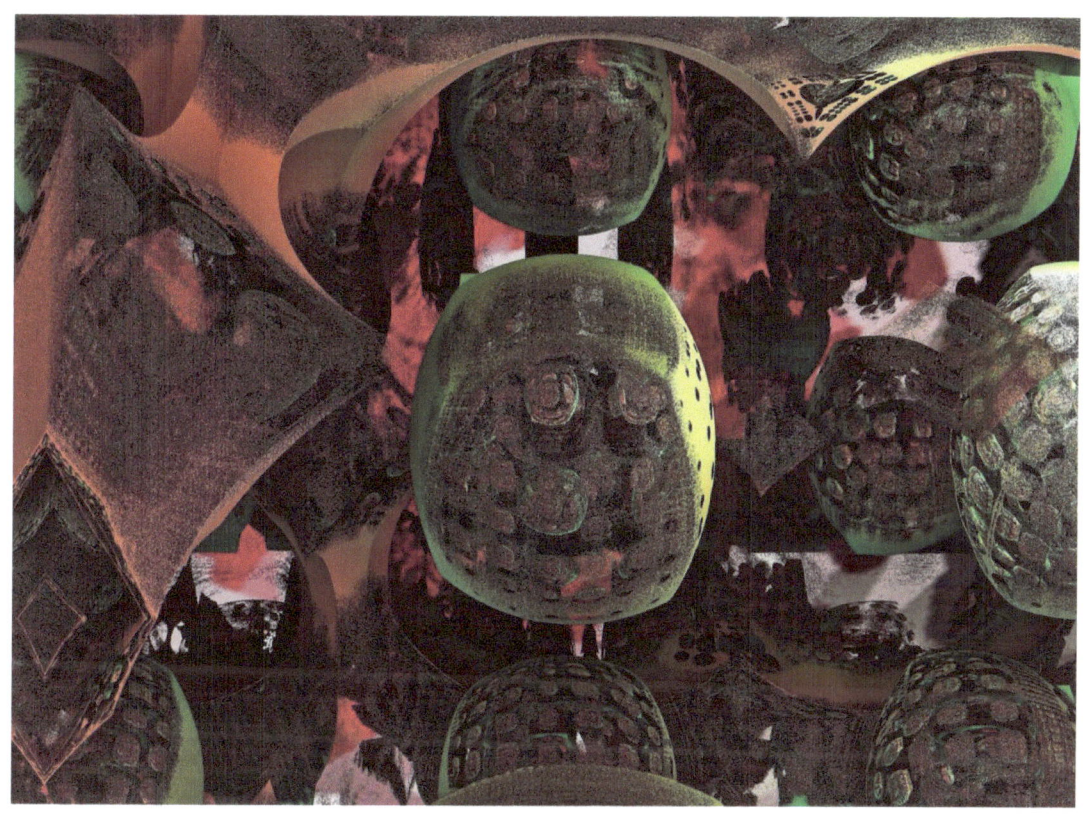

Seeds of Creation

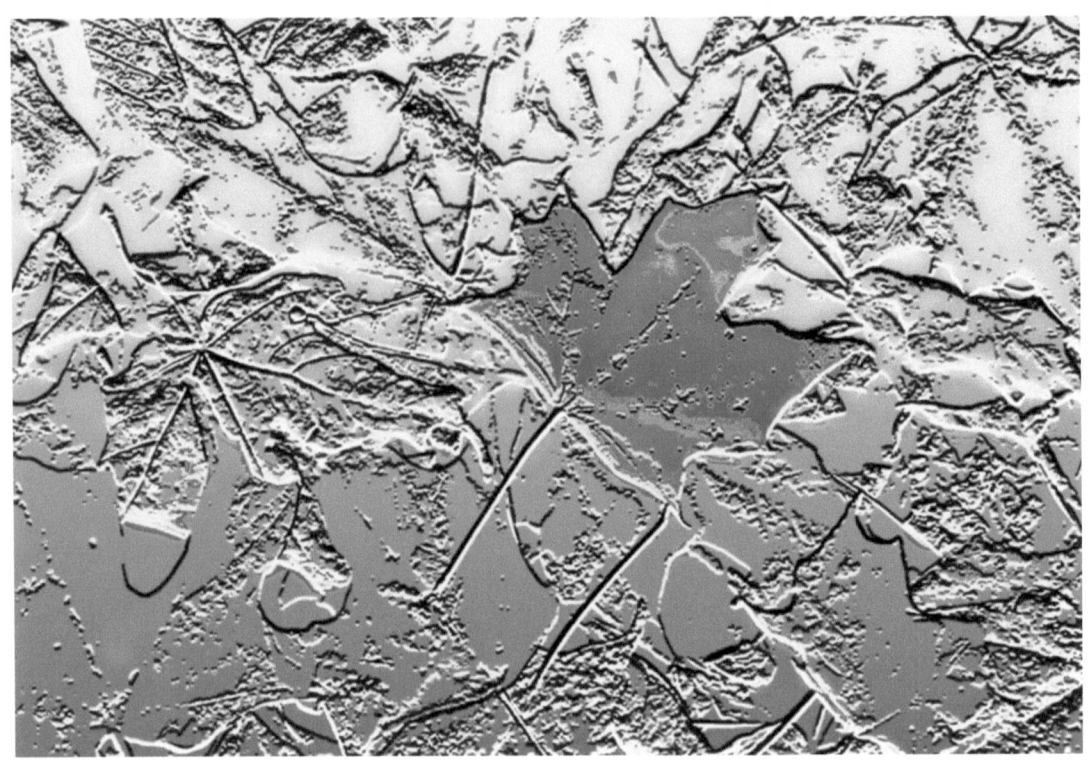

Frozen Memory of Fall

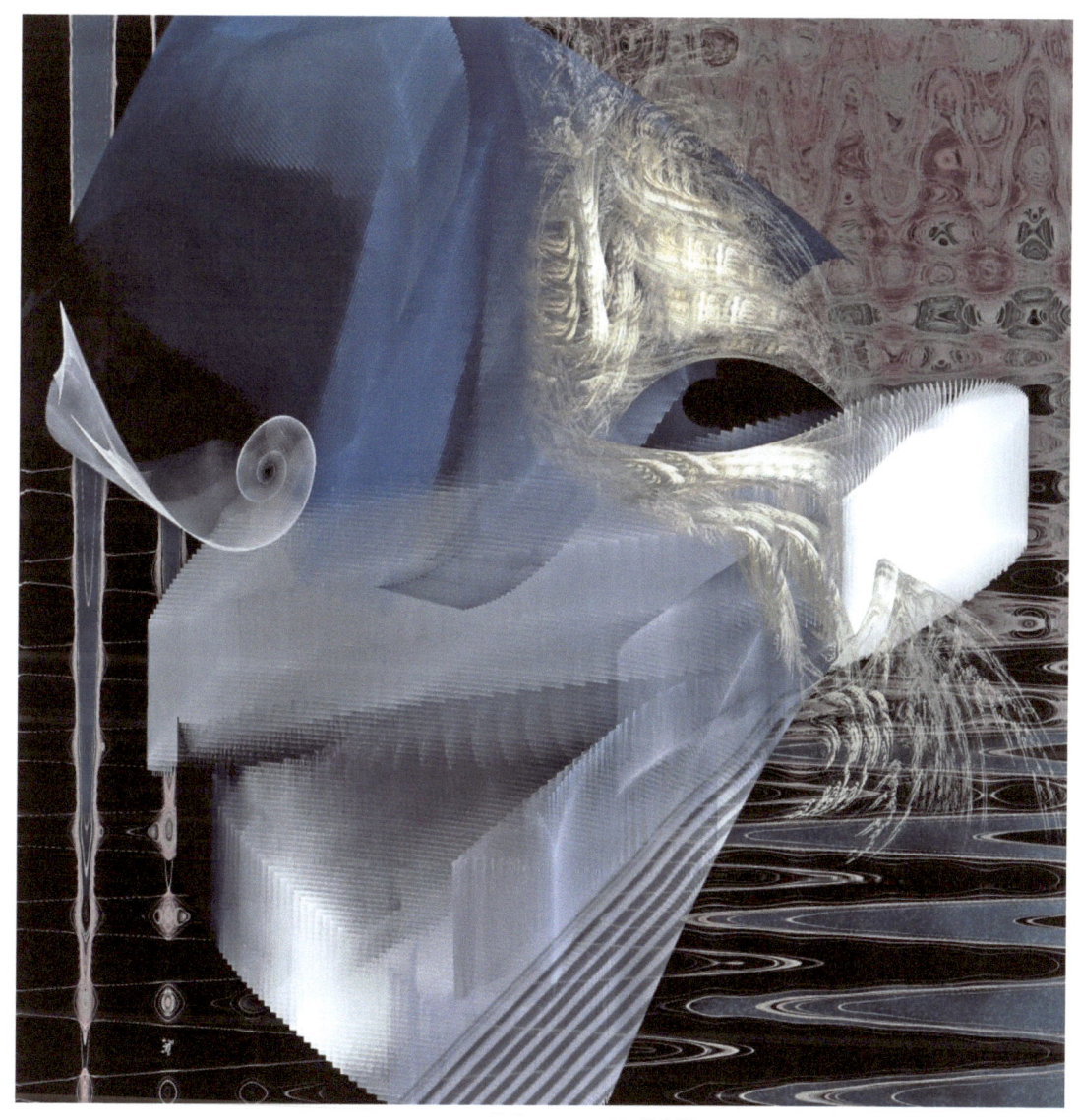

Masked

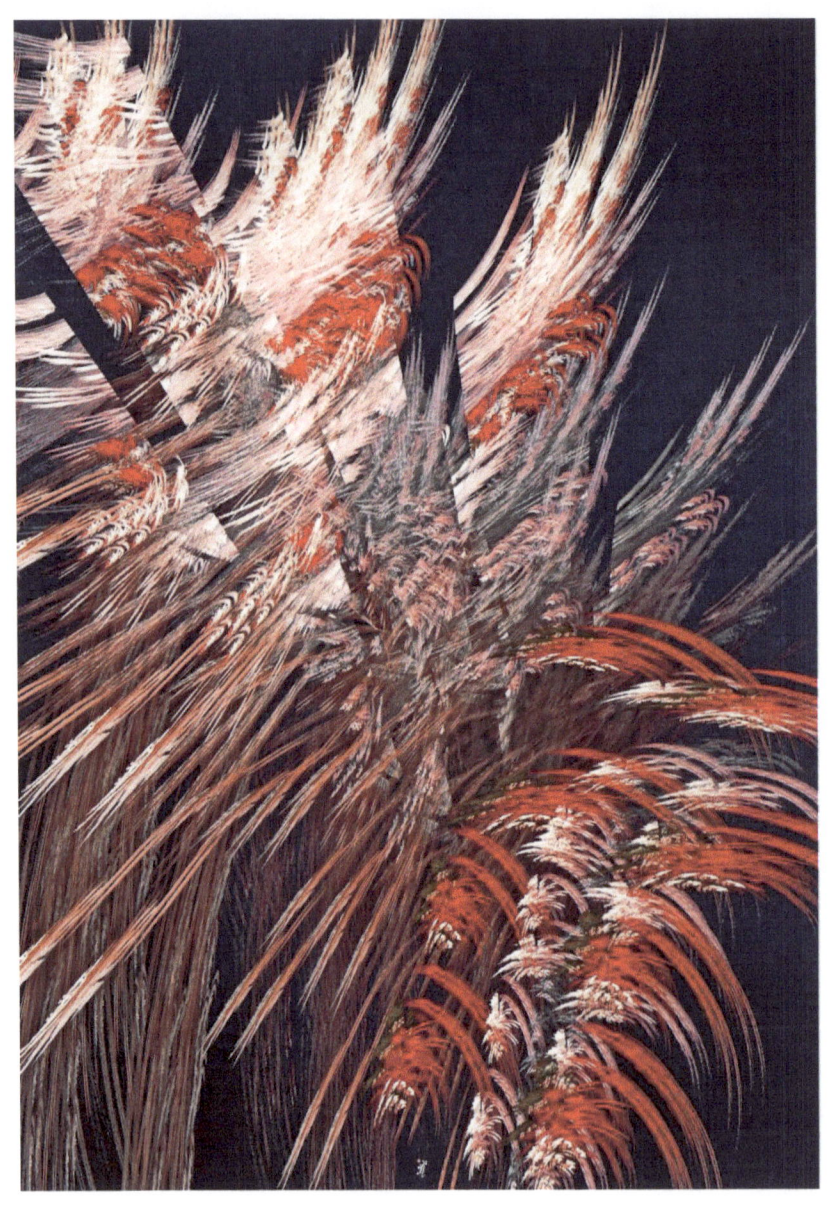

Celebration

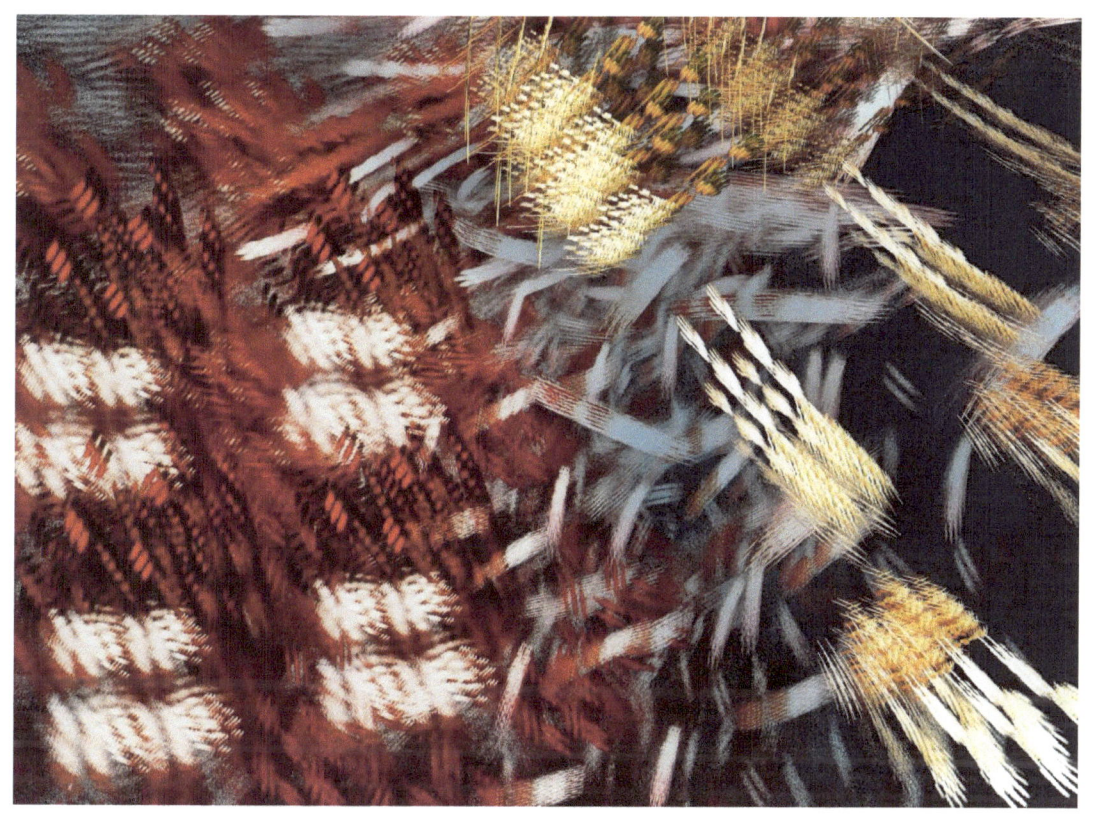

Weavings

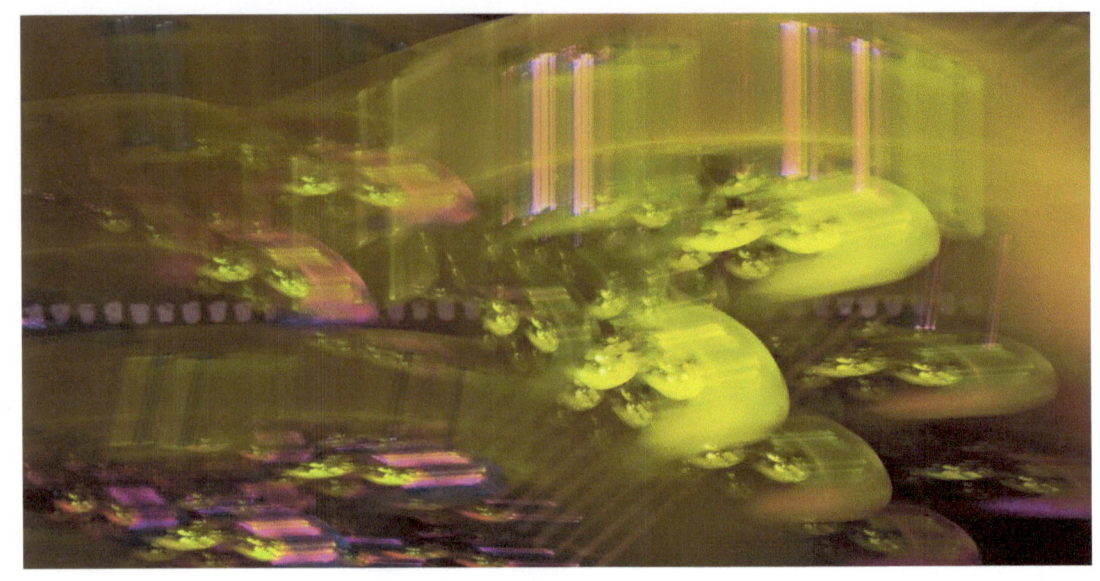

Treasure

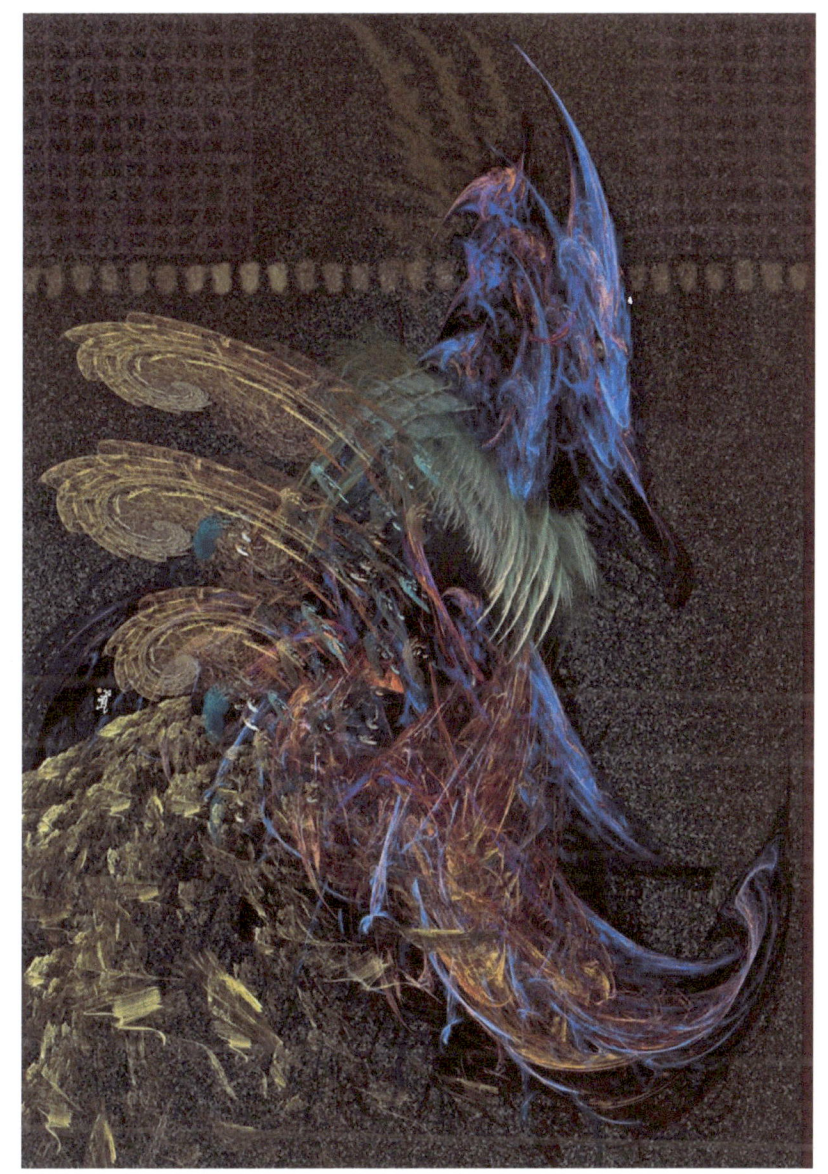

Wild and Beautiful Bird

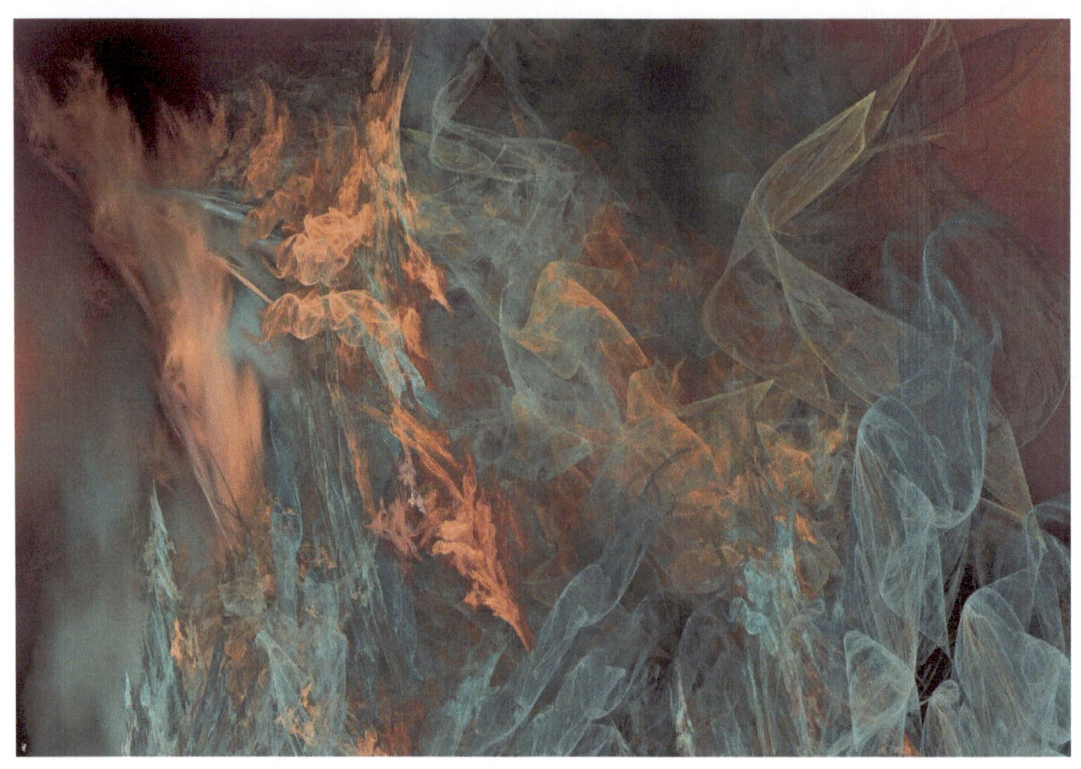

Where there is Smoke

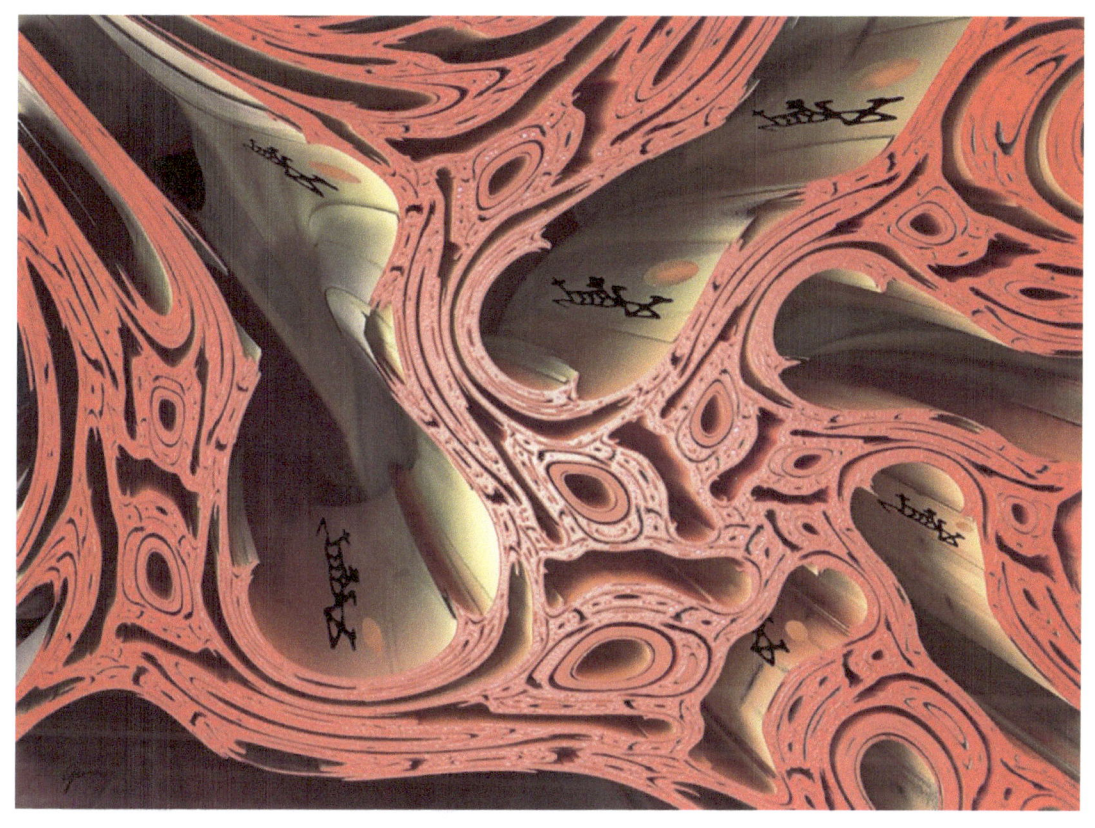

Written in Blood on Bone

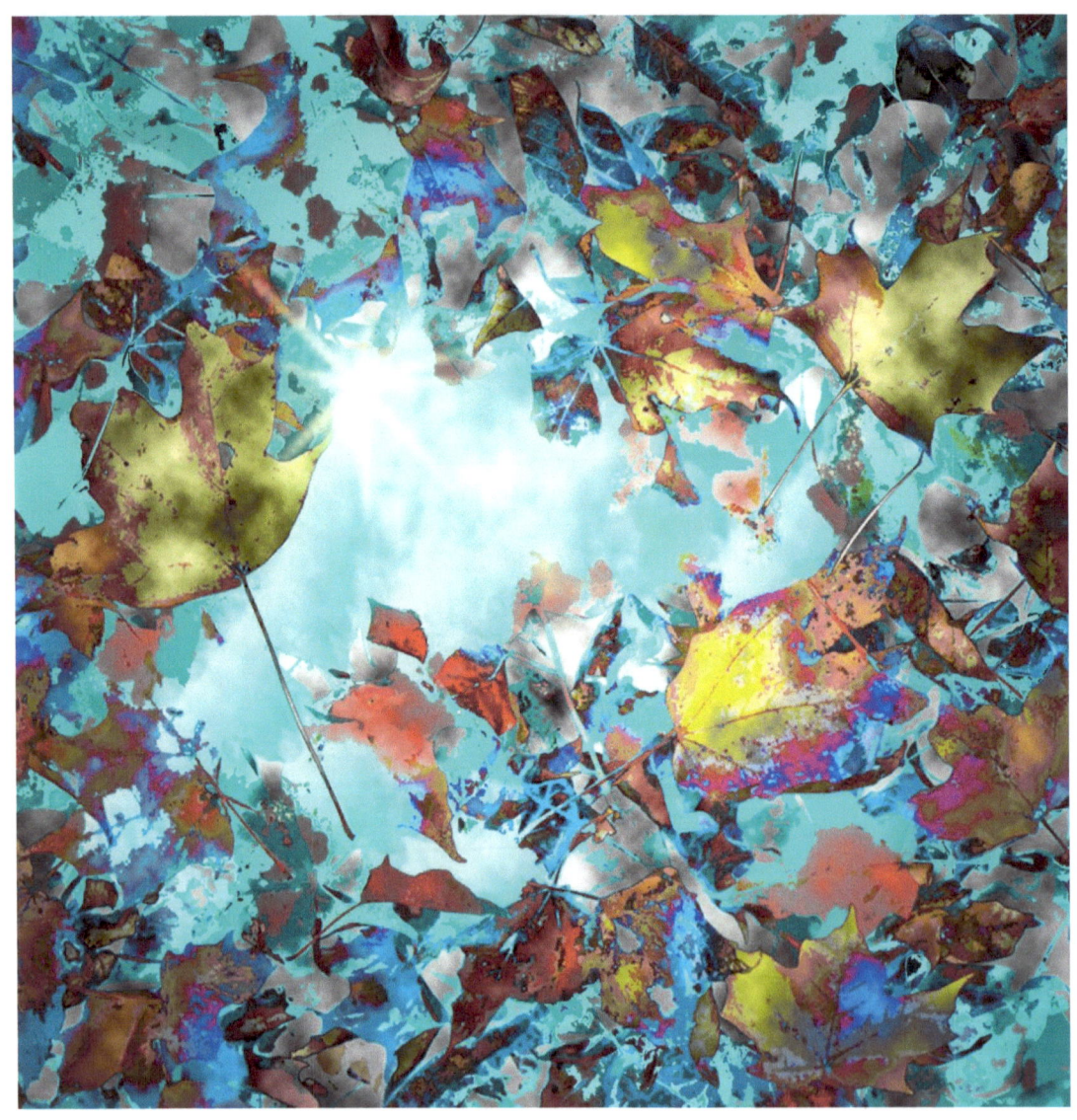

View of the Sky from the Bottom of the Pond

40

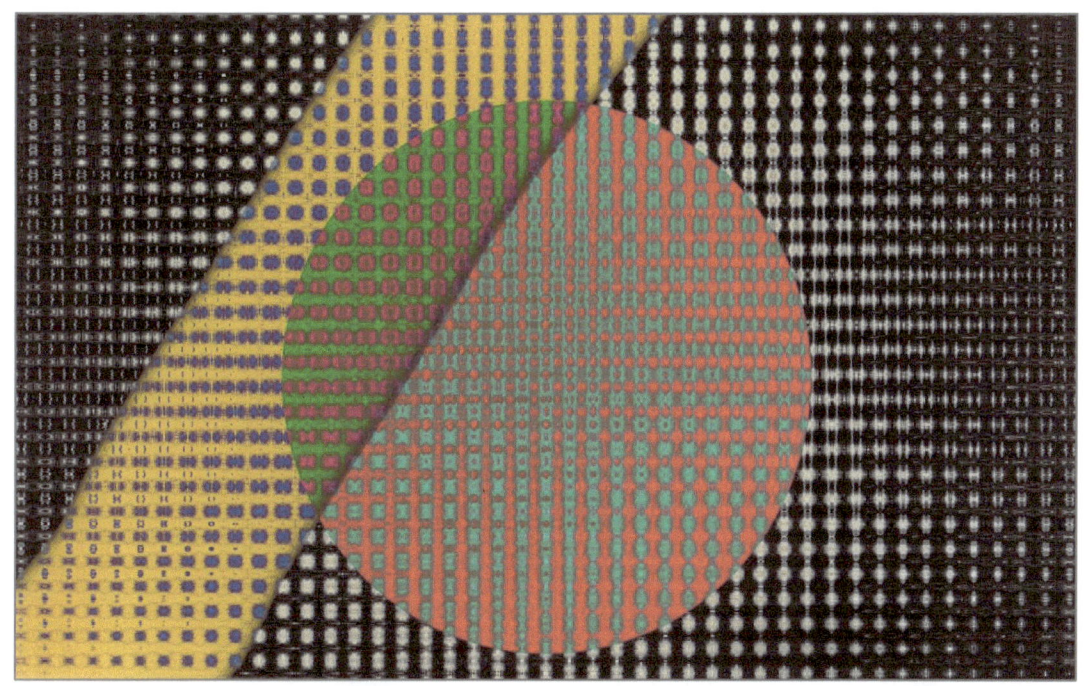

Solar Radiation

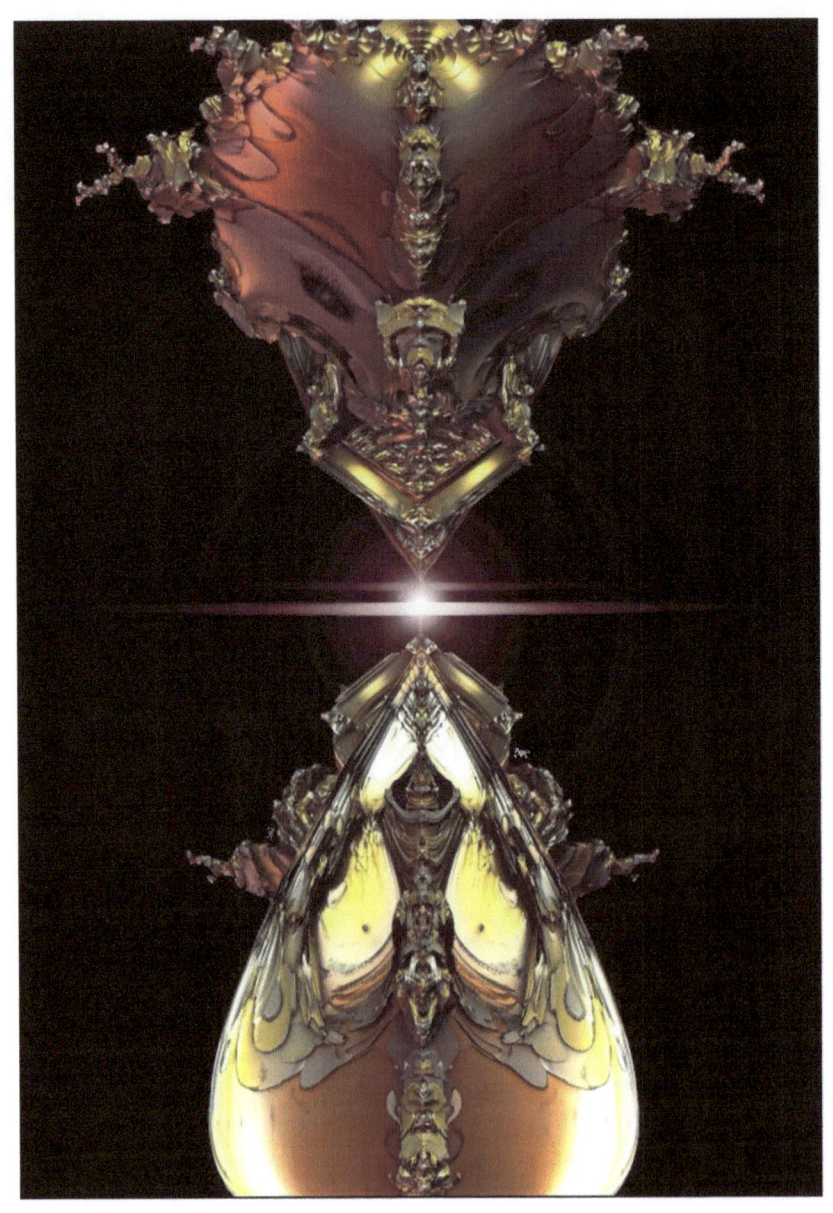

Soul Reflection

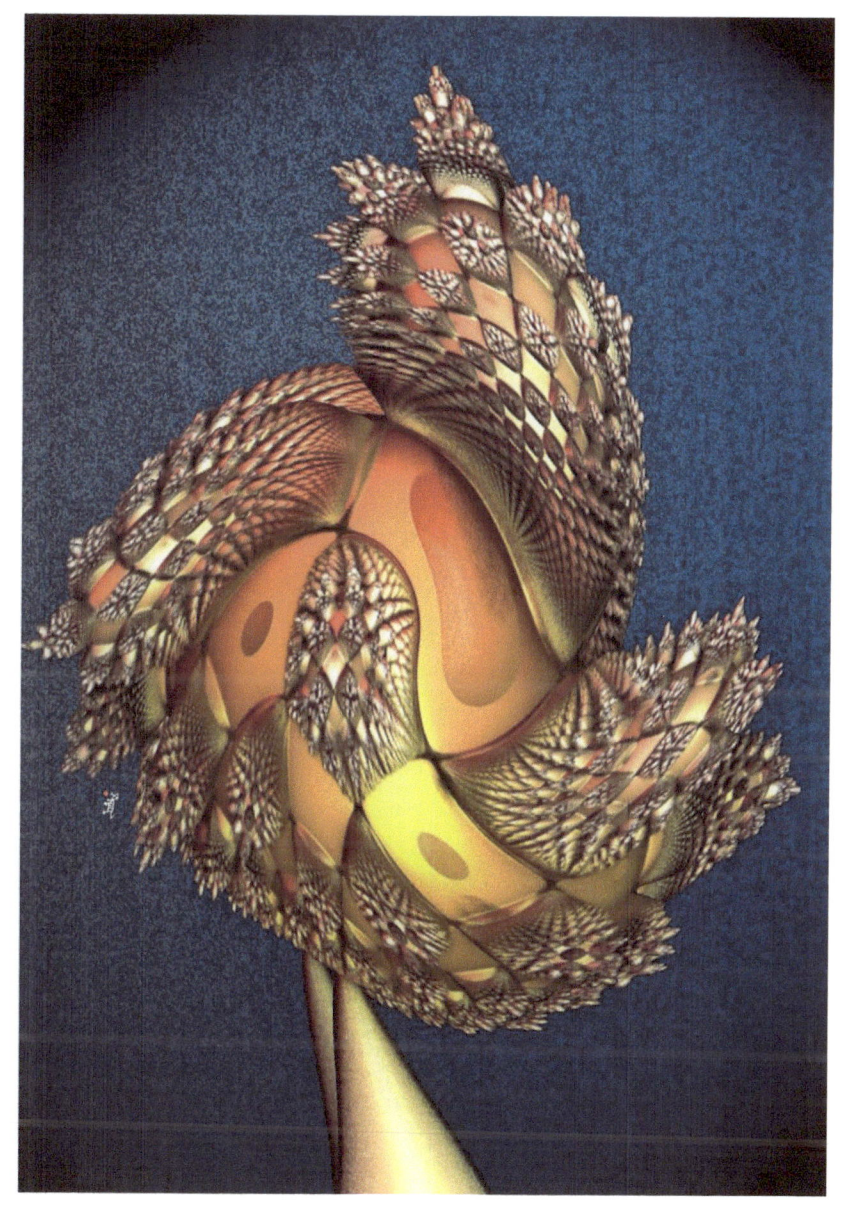

Spotlight on the Dance

43

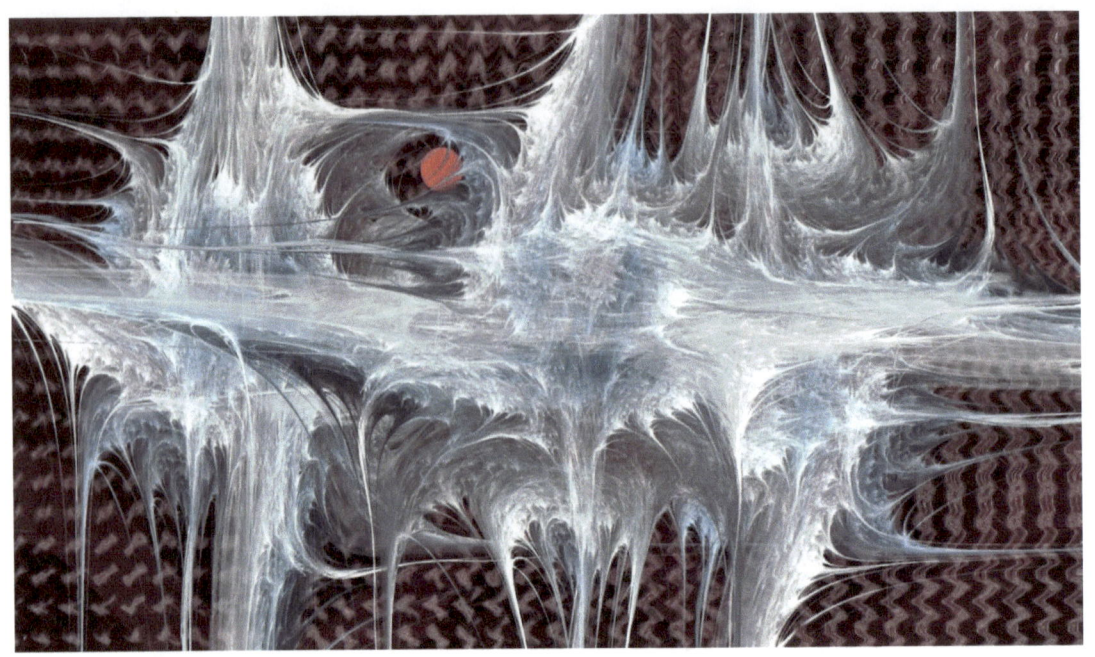

Splash

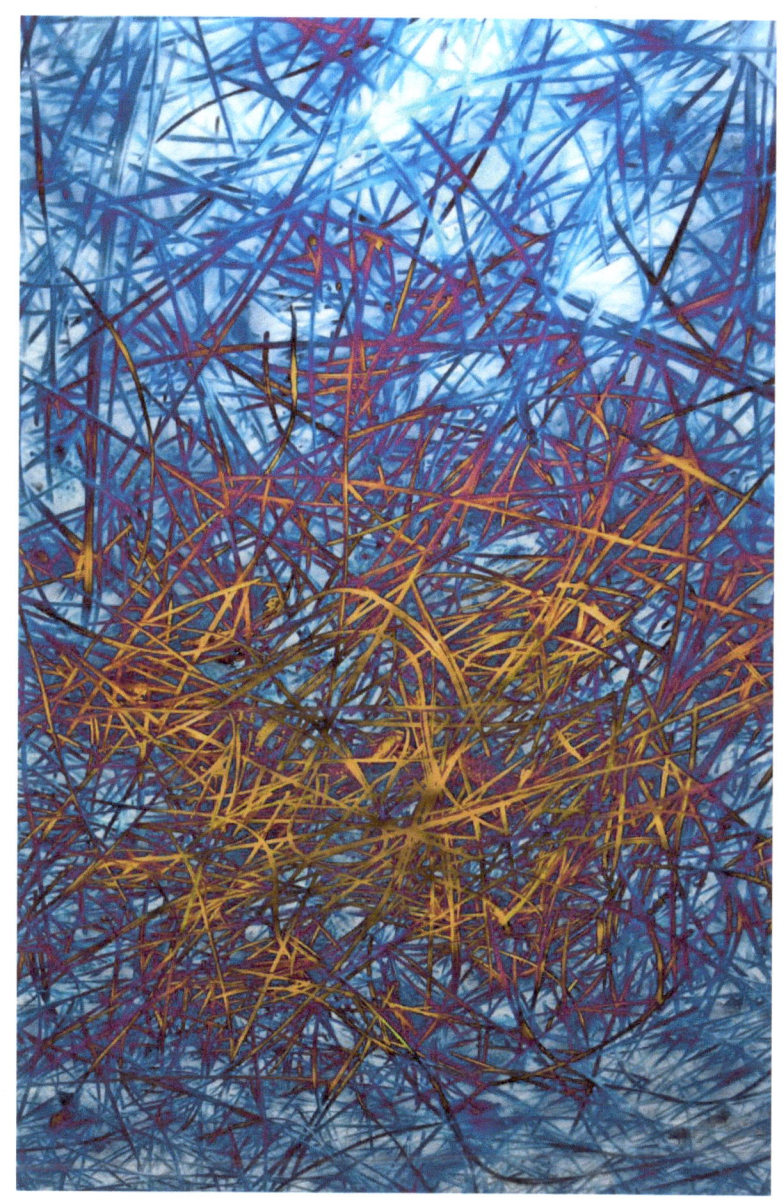

Under the Seaweed

45

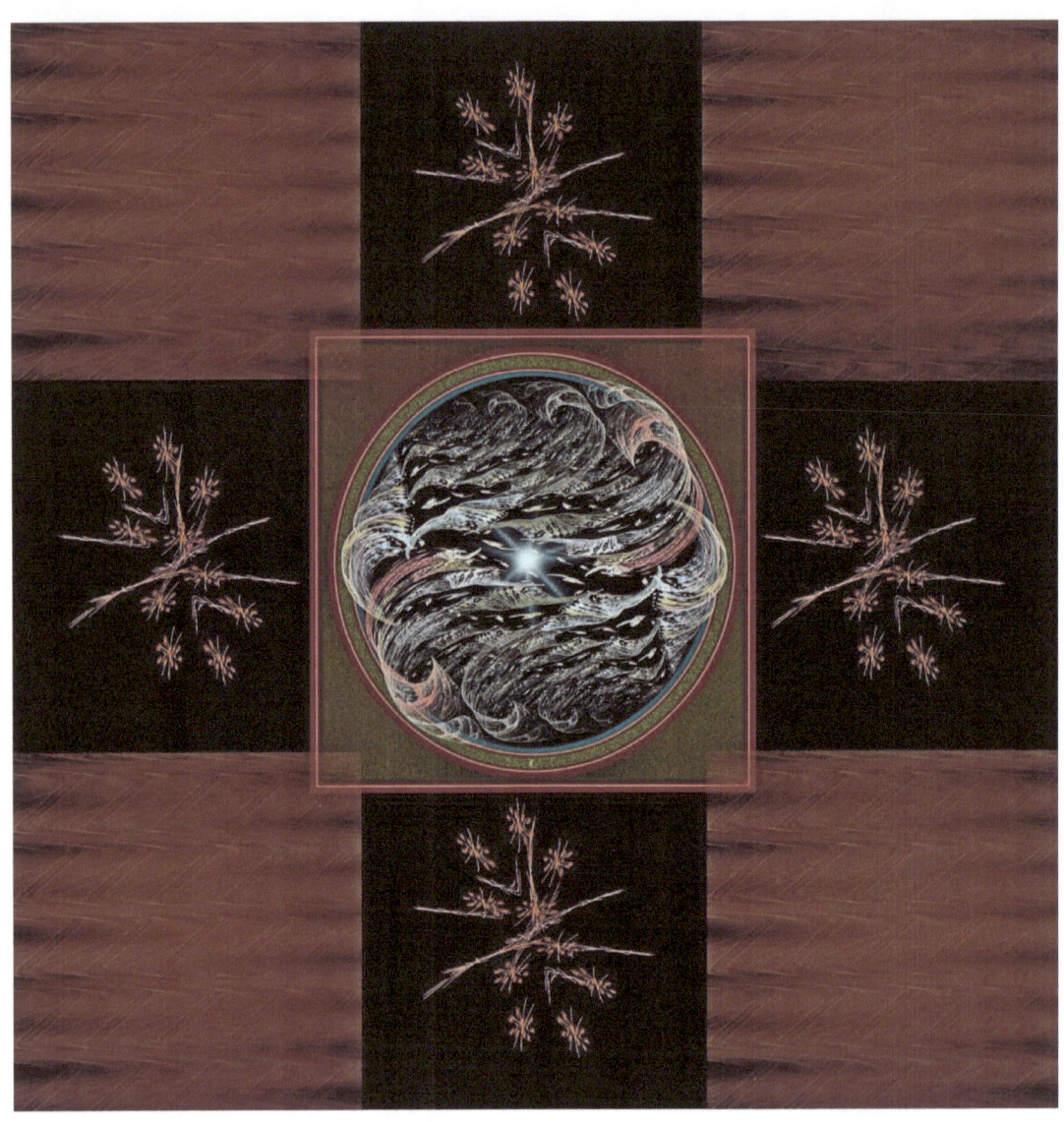

Eternal Sea

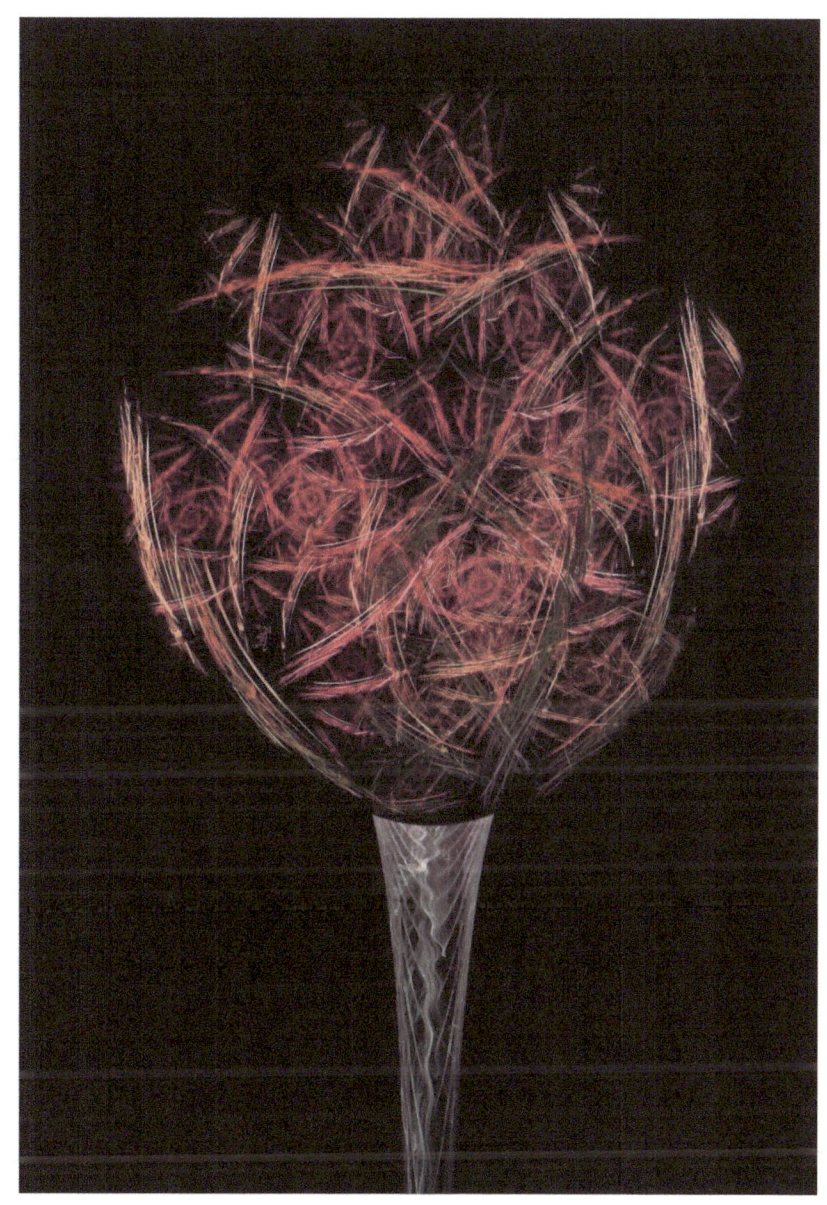

Essence

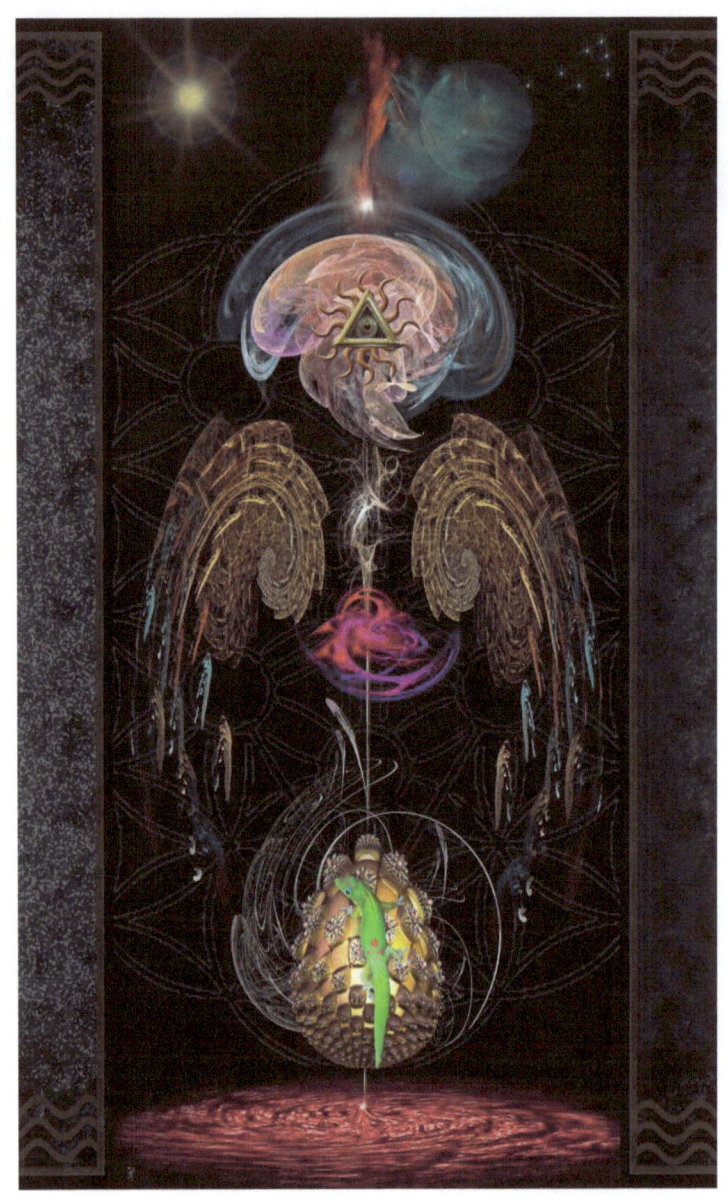

Anatomy

48

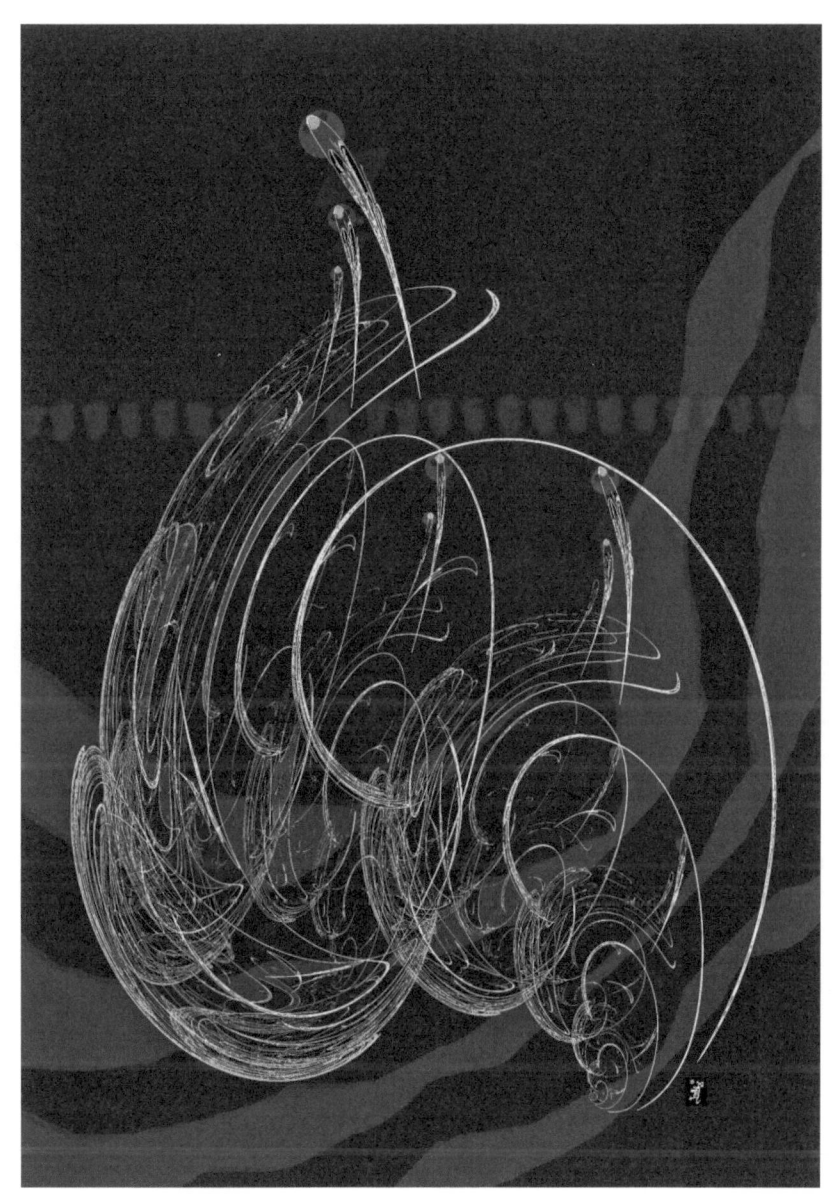

The Human Gene Pool

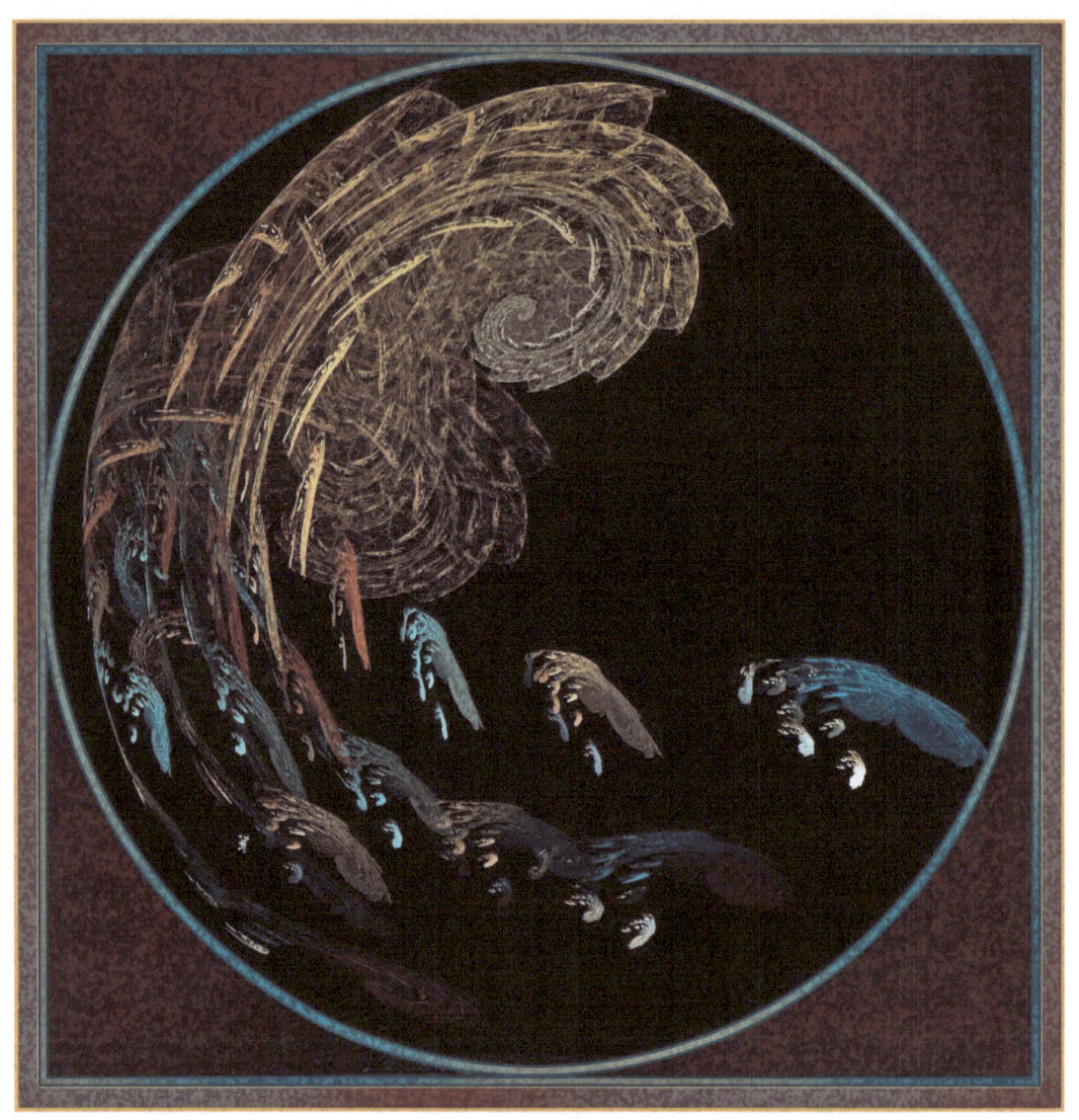

Ocean Life

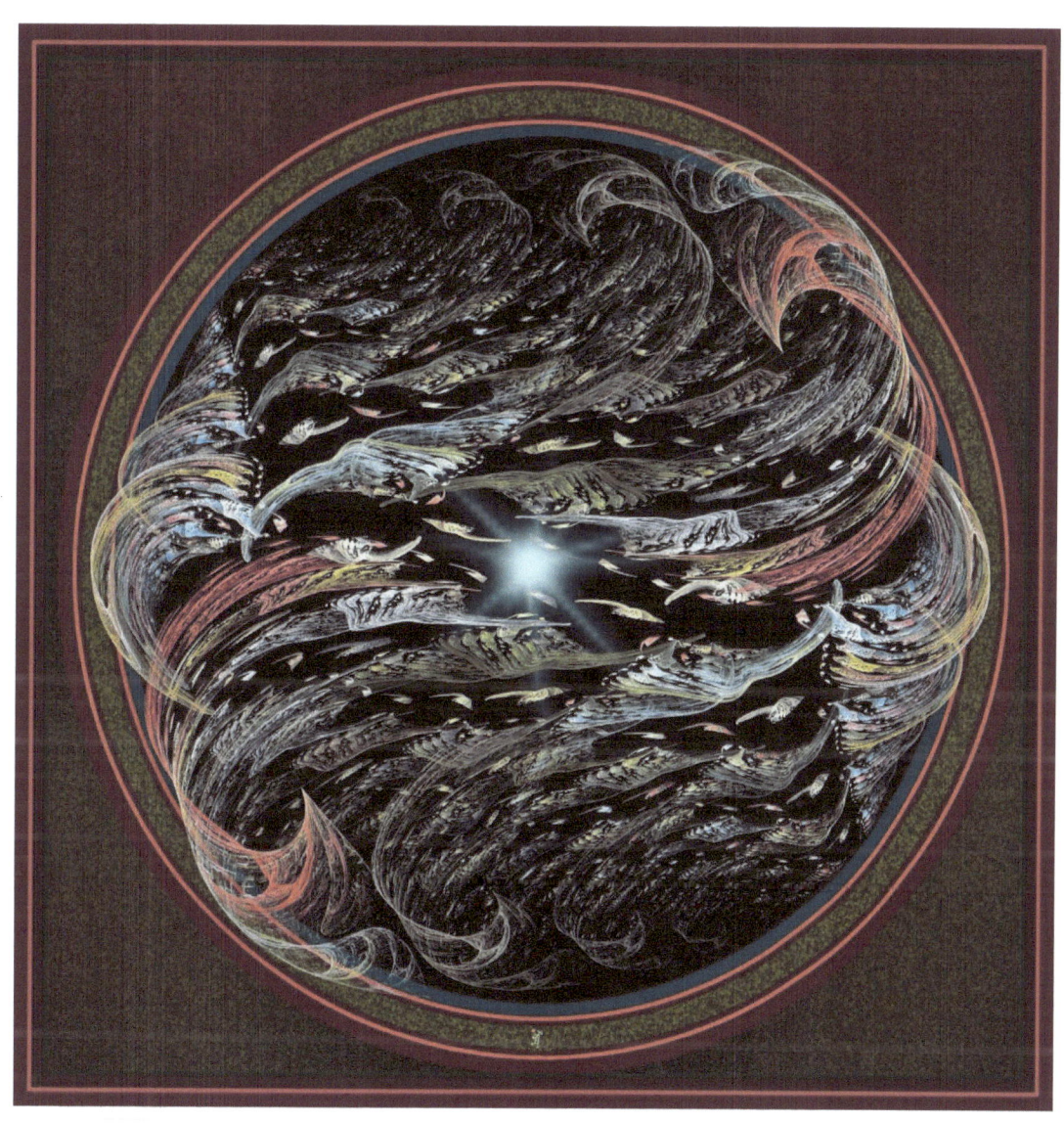

Center of the Eternal Sea

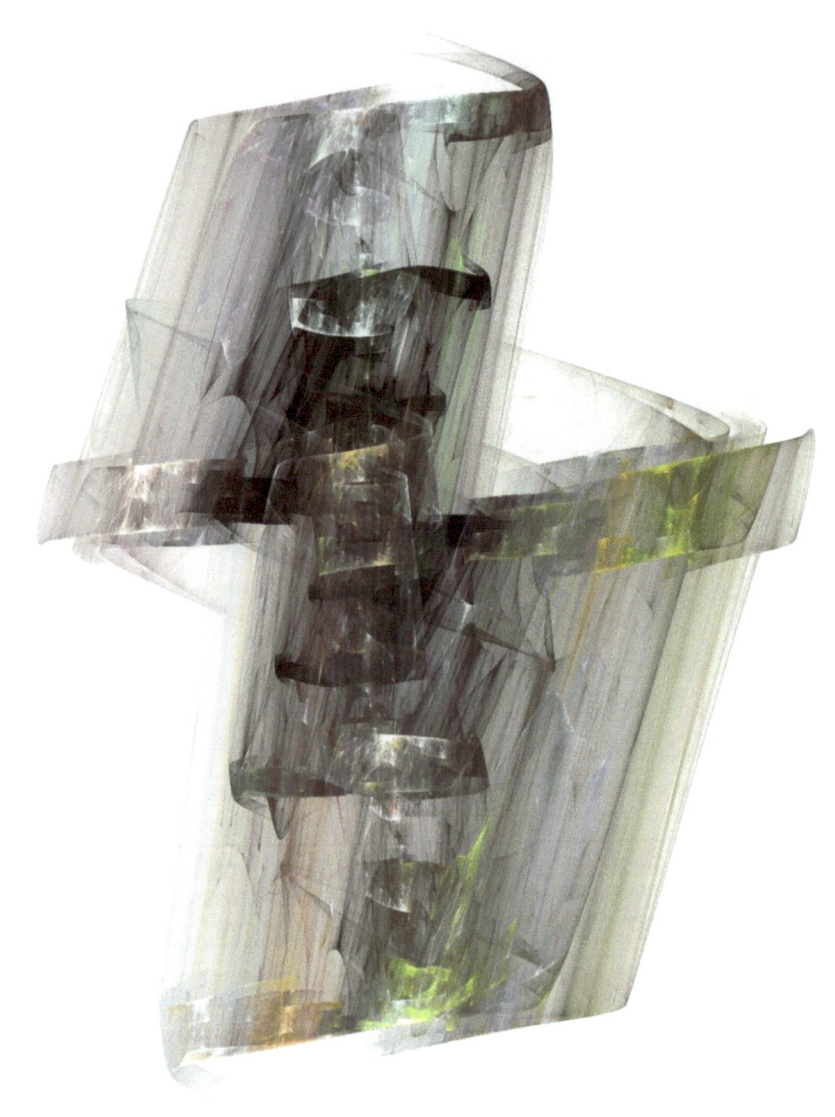

Glass and Steel

52

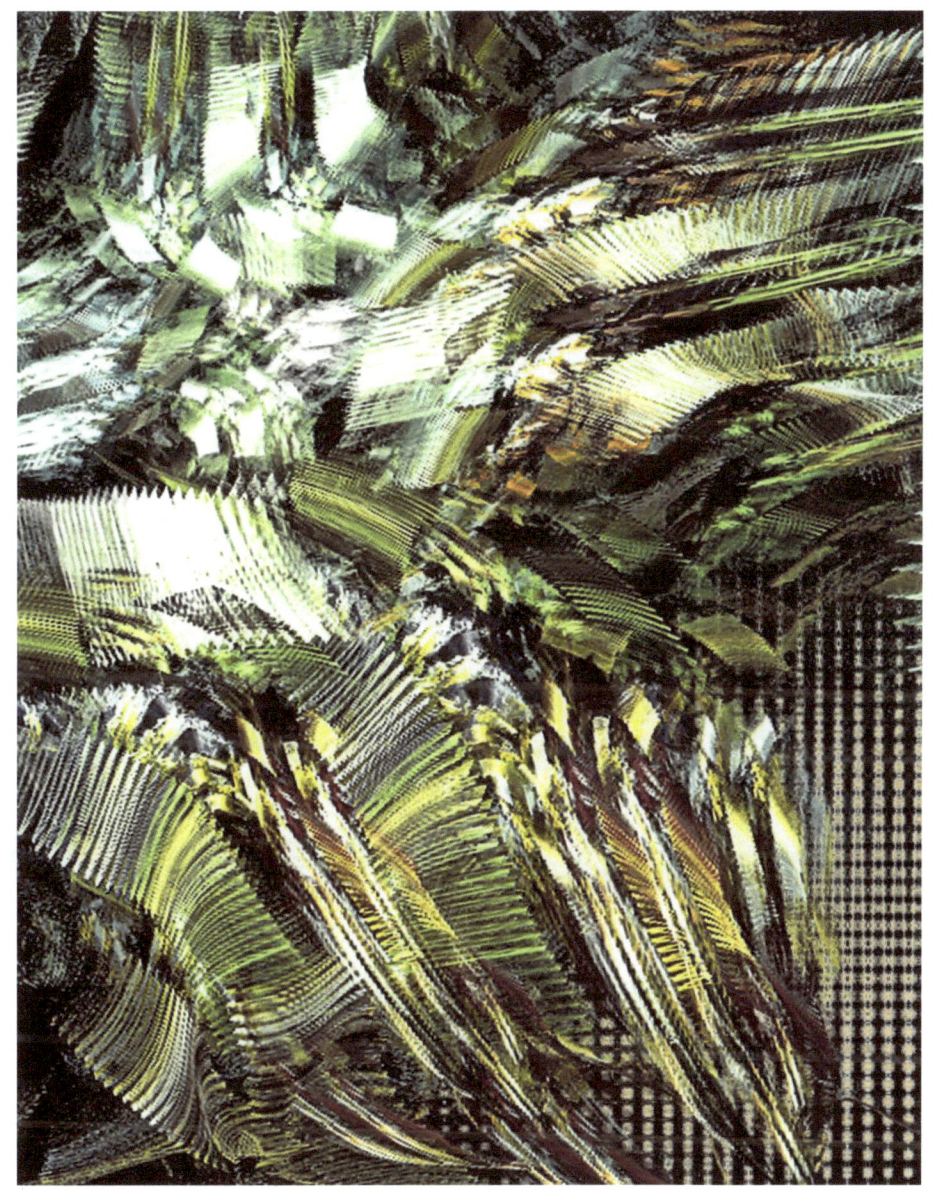

Steel Shavings

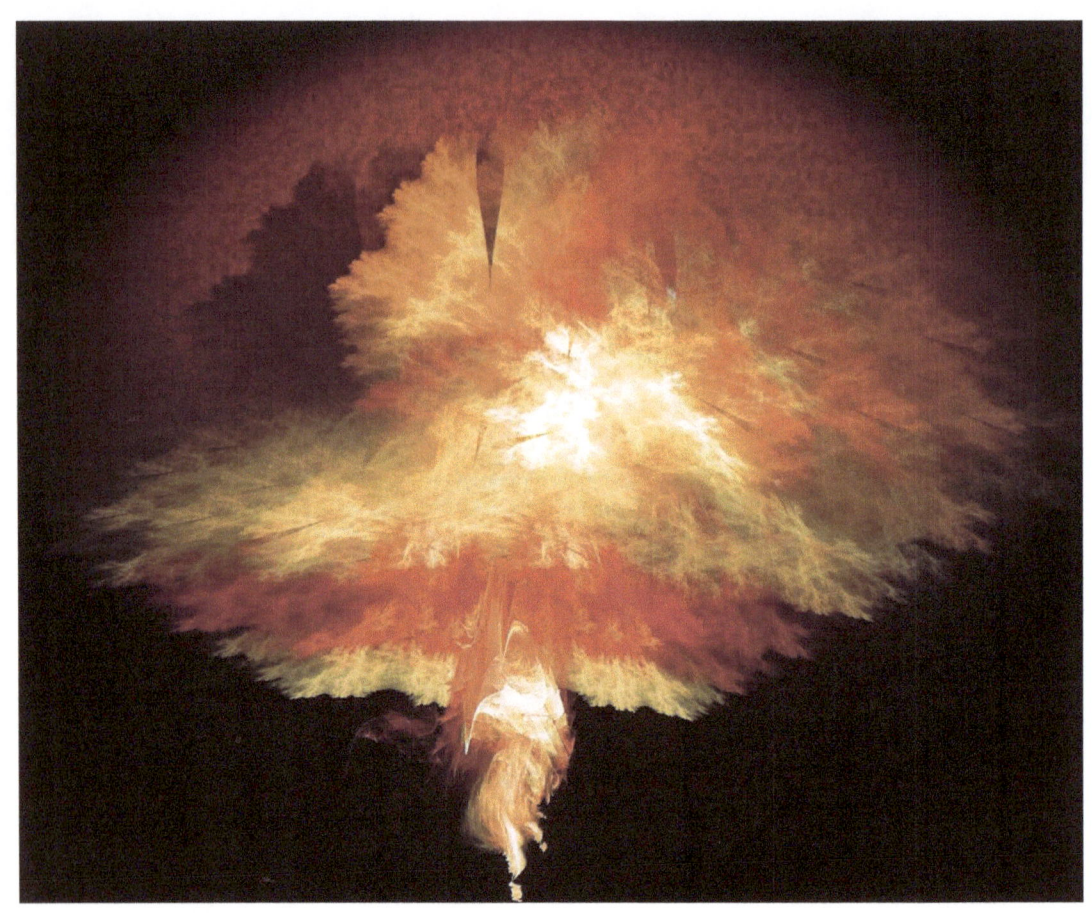

Fractal Explosion

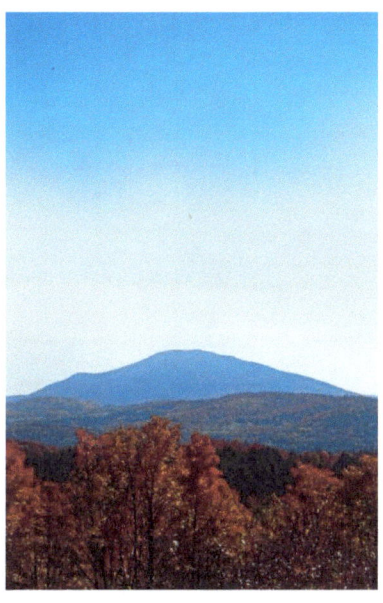

Located high in the hills of rural New England, on a winding country road, just like you, we enjoy the global reach of the world-wide web. Inquiries regarding signed original paintings or archival quality limited edition prints are welcome.

www.GloriaKingMerritt.com

www.ingramcontent.com/pod-product-compliance
Lightning Source LLC
Chambersburg PA
CBHW050810180526
45159CB00004B/1616